UNDERSTANDING RHETORIC

A Graphic Guide to WRITING

Elizabeth Losh
Jonathan Alexander
Kevin Cannon
Zander Cannon

BEDFORD / ST. MARTIN'S

BOSTON • NEW YORK

For Bedford/St. Martin's

Senior Executive Editor: Leasa Burton
Executive Editor: Carolyn Lengel
Senior Production Editor: Deborah Baker
Senior Production Supervisor: Jennifer Peterson
Executive Marketing Manager: Molly Parke
Editorial Assistants: Daniel Schafer, Leah Rang
Copy Editor: Arthur Johnson
Indexer: Mary White
Permissions Manager: Kalina K. Ingham
Senior Art Director: Anna Palchik
Cover Illustrators: Kevin Cannon, Zander Cannon
Printing and Binding: RR Donnelley and Sons

President, Bedford/St. Martin's: Denise B. Wydra
Presidents, Macmillan Higher Education: Joan E. Feinberg and Tom Scotty
Editor in Chief: Karen S. Henry
Director of Development: Erica T. Appel
Director of Marketing: Karen R. Soeltz
Production Director: Susan W. Brown
Associate Production Director: Elise S. Kaiser
Managing Editor: Elizabeth Schaaf

Manufactured in the United States of America.
8 7 6 5 4 3
f e d c b a

For information, write: Bedford/St. Martin's, 75 Arlington Street, Boston, MA 02116
   (617-399-4000)

ISBN 978-0-312-64096-5

Acknowledgments

Acknowledgments and copyrights appear at the back of the book on page 277, which constitutes an extension of the copyright page. It is a violation of the law to reproduce these selections by any means whatsoever without the written permission of the copyright holder.

CONTENTS

Contents

PREFACE: GETTING GRAPHIC

Understanding Rhetoric is the work of many hands and many years—a project that attempts to combine some of the best knowledge and practices from the teaching of writing with a forward-thinking approach to visual and multimodal literacy.

You'll find that this book covers all the commonly taught topics in first-year composition, offering time-tested techniques for improving critical analysis, argumentation, and the development of research questions in college writing. It contains practical tips for improving organization, identifying bias, evaluating sources, representing scholarly debates, and avoiding plagiarism.

It also reflects the latest research in composition, which focuses on the development of writers as well as writing.

In short, this is an effective classroom text that is thoroughly grounded in scholarship.

But perhaps the most unusual feature of this book—the one that you can't help noticing—is that this is a comic book. When we began to work on this book, we hoped that by emphasizing multimodal approaches to composing, we would engage student writers in thinking about their identities, contexts for their research, and effective writing processes. But we also wanted to create a book that students would actually want to read—a book that could make rhetoric interesting and maybe even enjoyable.

"ENGAGING AND LIGHTHEARTED, BUT ALSO CAREFULLY ORGANIZED, THEORETICALLY SOUND, AND A COMPELLING WAY TO TEACH STUDENTS ABOUT CRITICAL READING AND WRITING IN A TECHNOLOGICALLY ADVANCED, INFORMATION-RICH SOCIETY."

Michael Pemberton,
Georgia Southern University

Increasingly, composition instructors recognize that students need a range of literacy skills. The Web, video, blogging, YouTube, Tumblr, and social network sites complement and challenge traditional text-based literacy practices, and students must consider the rhetorical requirements of writing for multimodal platforms and also think about graphic design and visual evidence as part of their basic tools for communication. After all, many of them may be doing most of their writing using such platforms.

Many writing instructors have begun using comics in the composition classroom to engage students with writing that is both textually and visually rich. The visual dimension of the text doesn't simply illustrate rhetorical concepts; rather, the images and text must be read in tandem for the reader to fully grasp the concepts being discussed. In composing *Understanding Rhetoric*, we decided to capitalize on such pedagogical energy by talking about rhetoric in the medium of a graphic book.

Understanding Rhetoric is arranged into eight "issues" dealing with particular rhetorical concepts, each using a different accent color.

- Every issue begins with a chapter featuring somewhat hyperbolic versions of "Liz and Jonathan," who interact with historical and comic-book characters (and with illustrators and coauthors Kevin Cannon and Zander Cannon). Most chapters include a quick-reference chart recapping important ideas.
- A "ReFrame" section after each chapter features two student characters, Luis and Cindy, grappling with that chapter's concepts and "walking through" one of a variety of texts.
- A "Drawing Conclusions" spread at the end of each issue suggests assignments that will allow students to try the concepts out for themselves.

"A HIP, CONTEMPORARY, AND WITTY EXPLANATION OF THE HISTORY AND SIGNIFICANCE OF RHETORIC FOR THE DIGITAL AGE."

Adam Bessie,
Diablo Valley College

"THIS TEXT IS FUN. IT MAKES PEOPLE WANT TO COME BACK TO THE IDEAS AGAIN AND AGAIN."

Chris Gerben,
Stanford University

As you read through the text with your classes, ask students to pay attention not only to what the characters are saying, but to how information about writing and composing is conveyed both textually and visually. Our hands-on style emphasizes an active approach to writing, reading, and responding to all kinds of texts and emphasizes the dialogic nature of successful academic and public writing.

Ultimately, to enter into conversations (in good Burkean fashion) in different public spheres, writers should work through a series of interactions and discussions that allow them to craft insightful positions and compelling arguments. Our characters show how all writing is connected to identities. People write from particular positions, stances, and senses of self, and having a greater awareness of those positions—social, cultural, political, and historical—makes for more sophisticated and assured composing.

We hope you and your students enjoy *Understanding Rhetoric*. We also invite you to check out the instructor's manual and Student Site for further samples and teaching ideas, along with information about how our book supports the Council of Writing Program Administrators (WPA) Outcomes, at **bedfordstmartins.com/understandingrhetoric**.

Ginger Jurecka Blake,
University of Wisconsin

Most importantly, feel free as you teach with this book to talk back to us. Dare to disagree, either with us or other characters in the book. Get graphic with the text, and invite your students to draw and write within it. You might find yourself working with your students to make your own graphic guide to writing!

AUTHOR ACKNOWLEDGMENTS

We appreciate the contributions of the many, many individuals whose expertise and advice made this book possible.

Reviewers

We received invaluable feedback from a wonderful group of reviewers, whose suggestions helped us shape the direction of individual chapters and of the book as a whole during its entire development process: Tom Amorose, Seattle Pacific University; Max Badesheim III, Boise State University; Kim Ballard, Western Michigan University; Joseph Bartolotta, University of Minnesota; Diane Forbes Berthoud, University of California, San Diego; Adam Bessie, Diablo Valley College; Ginger Jurecka Blake, University of Wisconsin; Lady Branham, University of Oklahoma; Beth Buyserie, Washington State University; James "Bucky" Carter, University of Texas at El Paso; Christine Cucciarre, University of Delaware; Kathryn E. Dobson, McDaniel College; Sergio C. Figueiredo, Clemson University; John Garrison, University of California, Davis; Oriana Gatta, Georgia State University; Chris Gerben, Stanford University; Mathew Gomes, California State University, Fresno; Jim Haendiges, Dixie State College of Utah; Levia Hayes, College of Southern Nevada; Fred Johnson, Whitworth University; Jeraldine Kraver, University of Northern Colorado; Nate Kreuter, Western Carolina University; Bradley Lane, North Seattle Community College; Matthew Levy, Pacific Lutheran University; Kelli Moore, University of California, San Diego; Shannon R. Mortimore-Smith, Shippensburg

University; Michael Pemberton, Georgia Southern University; Erin Presley, University of Georgia; Scott Reed, University of Georgia; Molly Scanlon, Virginia Tech; Cheri Lemieux Spiegel, Northern Virginia Community College; Michael Sutcliffe, Washington State University Vancouver; Phil Troutman, George Washington University; Christopher Werry, San Diego State University; Alan Williams, Illinois State University; and Joseph Willis, Southern Utah University.

Contributors
We would like to acknowledge some of the people who helped in the creation of this book by sharing their ideas about writing and rhetoric: Norah Ashe, University of Southern California; Greg Benford, University of California, Irvine; Vinayak Chaturvedi, University of California, Irvine; Michael Clark, University of California, Irvine; James Paul Gee, Arizona State University; Brook Haley, University of California, Irvine; Michael Householder, Southern Methodist University; Julia Lupton, University of California, Irvine; Steven Mailloux, Loyola Marymount University; Lynn Malley, University of California, Irvine; Michele Mason, University of Maryland; Robert Moeller, University of California, Irvine; Erika Nanes, University of Southern California; Ellen Strenski; Brook Thomas, University of California, Irvine; Phil Troutman, George Washington University; and Ann Van Sant, University of California, Irvine.

For allowing us to adapt a paragraph from her student essay on Japanese Americans in internment camps during World War II, many thanks to Marissa Osato, a graduate of the University of California, Irvine.

Author Acknowledgments

For contributions to our thinking on the instructor's manual for *Understanding Rhetoric*, our gratitude goes to Henry Jenkins, Keith McCleary, Emily Roxworthy, Molly Scanlon, Cynthia Selfe, and Wayne Yang.

We thank Tom Gammill for his illustrations in Chapter 5.

We are grateful to Thomas LeBien of Hill & Wang and to Jessica Marshall of Eye Candy Books for helpful initial feedback on this project.

Finally, we would like to thank Zander Cannon and Kevin Cannon, our coauthors, for turning our manuscript into a real comic book. They contributed not just illustrations, but also many great ideas for conveying concepts visually—and a lot of good jokes.

Bedford/St. Martin's
Everyone on the team at Bedford/St. Martin's was critical for bringing this publication to fruition. Constructive and creative feedback—from Leasa Burton, Carolyn Lengel, Allie Goldstein, Daniel Schafer, Leah Rang, Karrin Varucene, Joan Feinberg, and Denise Wydra—over the course of many lively conversations was central to our writing process. We are grateful to Anna Palchik for her art direction; to our project editor, Deb Baker, and our copy editor, Arthur Johnson; to Karita dos Santos for market development; and to our marketing manager, Molly Parke.

Elizabeth Losh, *University of California, San Diego*
Jonathan Alexander, *University of California, Irvine*

We would like to thank everyone at Bedford/St. Martin's for their support, encouragement, and enthusiasm over the course of making this book. In particular we'd like to thank Leasa Burton and Carolyn Lengel for their vision and guidance in seeing this book through from an idea to a finished project, and we'd like to thank Anna Palchik and Deb Baker for their support on the art and technical end.

Big thanks also go out to our coauthors, Liz and Jonathan, for being nimble with their script and adaptable to the peculiarities of making a comic book, and to all the additional challenges of making that comic book informative and educational. Finally, we appreciate the support of Thomas LeBien, who recommended us as artists for *Understanding Rhetoric* in the first place.

Also, Zander would like to thank his wife Julie and their son Jin for their support and for making their home a happy place to return to at the end of the day.

Kevin Cannon
Zander Cannon

SPACES FOR WRITING

In this issue...

OFTEN, WHEN PEOPLE TALK ABOUT BEGINNING A WRITING PROJECT, THIS IS WHAT THEY THINK ABOUT:

THE BLANK PAGE.

IT'S A WAY TO VISUALIZE ISOLATION, SOLITUDE, AND LONELINESS; STRUGGLING WITH ONE'S SOUL IN A PRIVATE ROOM; AGONIZING OVER WORD AFTER WORD; DILIGENTLY WAITING FOR **INSPIRATION**!

OR THEY ARE AWASH IN IDEAS, INSIGHTS, AND OBSERVATIONS THAT CROWD OUT THEIR ABILITY TO THINK CLEARLY AND COMMUNICATE CONCISELY.

THERE'S SO MUCH TO SAY -- HOW DO YOU KNOW WHAT'S WORTH SAYING? AND WHEN TO SAY IT? AND HOW?

9

TO HELP YOU EXAMINE THE ELEMENTS OF THE WRITING SITUATION, MAKE SENSE OF THEM...

...TAKE ADVANTAGE OF THE OPPORTUNITIES THAT THEY PRESENT, AND AVOID THE PITFALLS...

...WE ARE USING BOTH IMAGES AND TEXT TO CONVEY OUR ADVICE.

WHAT WE'RE DOING IN THIS BOOK ISN'T ACTUALLY A NEW APPROACH.

IN FACT, NINETEENTH-CENTURY BOOKS ON RHETORIC OFTEN INCORPORATED ILLUSTRATIONS AND DIAGRAMS TO HELP THEIR READERS BECOME BETTER SPEAKERS AND WRITERS.

Gilbert Austin CHIRONOMIA SPHERE

We are simply taking this approach one step further, by bringing ourselves into the illustrations.

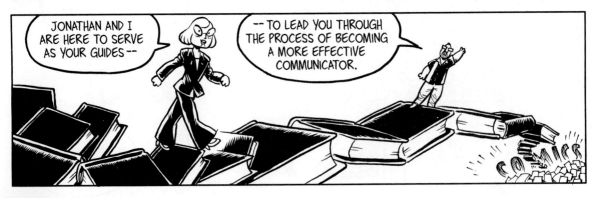

JONATHAN AND I ARE HERE TO SERVE AS YOUR GUIDES --

-- TO LEAD YOU THROUGH THE PROCESS OF BECOMING A MORE EFFECTIVE COMMUNICATOR.

GOING BOLDLY THROUGH WRITING PROCESSES

Introduction

...AND THAT MAY BE ONE OF THE MOST IMPORTANT LESSONS ABOUT LEARNING TO WRITE AND COMMUNICATE EFFECTIVELY.

PUSH PINS PUSH PINS

WHEN WE WERE WORKING ON THIS COMIC, FOR INSTANCE, WE KNEW THAT WE WOULD HAVE TO REVISE WHAT WE WROTE BASED ON WHAT THE ILLUSTRATORS DREW.

SOMETIMES KEVIN AND ZANDER DREW EXACTLY WHAT WE HAD IN MIND.

AND OTHER TIMES, THEY HAD **BETTER** IDEAS.

FAINT!

RHETORIC

UNCORRECTED PROOF

IF WE HADN'T ALL BEEN WILLING TO WORK WITH OTHERS' SUGGESTIONS, WE WOULD HAVE HAD A VERY LIMITED AND UNSATISFACTORY BOOK!

"Perfect manuscript"

SO WORKING COLLABORATIVELY FROM THE BEGINNING WAS A CRUCIAL COMPONENT OF OUR COMPOSING PROCESS.

AND NOW, BECAUSE WE ARE USING BOTH IMAGES AND WORDS TO CONVEY OUR ADVICE, WE WANT TO TO SAY SOMETHING ABOUT VISUAL LITERACY.

CONSIDER THIS: WHEN A PHOTOGRAPH APPEARS IN THE PAGES OF A GRAPHIC NOVEL, WE KNOW THAT IT HAS A SPECIAL SIGNIFICANCE.

IT LOOKS DIFFERENT FROM THE OTHER PICTURES ON THE PAGE.

IT SEEMS TO DEPICT MORE ACCURATELY THE WAY THAT SOMEONE OR SOMETHING LOOKS IN REAL LIFE.

SO, AT THIS MOMENT, A PERSON WHO OPENS TO THESE PAGES IN THIS BOOK CAN COMPARE THE APPEARANCE OF THE CARTOON ME TO THE ME OF THE PHOTOGRAPH.

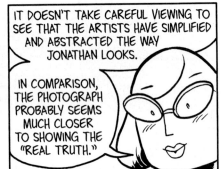

IT DOESN'T TAKE CAREFUL VIEWING TO SEE THAT THE ARTISTS HAVE SIMPLIFIED AND ABSTRACTED THE WAY JONATHAN LOOKS.

IN COMPARISON, THE PHOTOGRAPH PROBABLY SEEMS MUCH CLOSER TO SHOWING THE "REAL TRUTH."

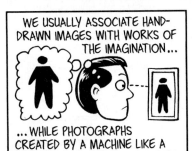

WE USUALLY ASSOCIATE HAND-DRAWN IMAGES WITH WORKS OF THE IMAGINATION...

...WHILE PHOTOGRAPHS CREATED BY A MACHINE LIKE A CAMERA ARE SUPPOSED TO GIVE US THE REAL STORY, THE FACTS.

HOWEVER, WE KNOW THAT, JUST LIKE A DRAWING, A PHOTOGRAPH IS REALLY ONLY A REPRESENTATION.

AFTER ALL, I CAN'T REACH IN AND ACTUALLY TOUCH THIS DESK.

MAYBE *I* CAN.

BUT THE READER CAN'T. IT'S A STATIC IMAGE THAT EXISTS ONLY IN TWO DIMENSIONS ON THE PAGE.

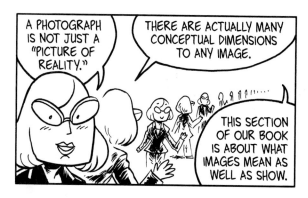

A PHOTOGRAPH IS NOT JUST A "PICTURE OF REALITY."

THERE ARE ACTUALLY MANY CONCEPTUAL DIMENSIONS TO ANY IMAGE.

THIS SECTION OF OUR BOOK IS ABOUT WHAT IMAGES MEAN AS WELL AS SHOW.

I WONDER WHAT THOSE STUDENTS ARE LAUGHING ABOUT?

JUST ADDING WORDS CAN CHANGE THE ENTIRE MEANING OF AN IMAGE.

AND THE FRAMING OF THE CONTENT MATTERS, TOO.

FOR EXAMPLE, WHEN AN IMAGE IS CROPPED IN A CERTAIN WAY, OR WHEN AN ILLUSTRATION SHOWS A DETAIL INSTEAD OF ZOOMING OUT TO SHOW A BIGGER PICTURE, THE ENTIRE MEANING OF THE IMAGE CAN CHANGE.

IN THIS VERSION, WE DON'T SEE A PROFESSIONAL SETTING.

THE IMAGE SENDS A VERY DIFFERENT MESSAGE WITHOUT THE OFFICIAL AND IMPOSING BACK-DROP OF AN OFFICE.

THEN, IF WE SEE MORE INFORMATION IN THE FRAME, THE MEANING CHANGES YET AGAIN.

THIS VERSION OF THE IMAGE IS MUCH MORE PLAYFUL AND SUBVERSIVE.

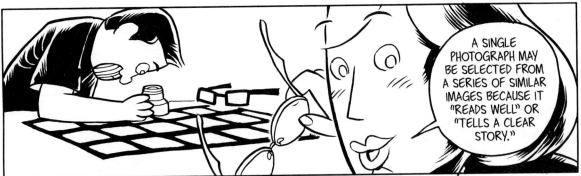

LEARNING TO READ THE DIFFERENT ELEMENTS OF A VISUAL TEXT IS PART OF WHAT WE CALL VISUAL LITERACY.

VISUAL LITERACY IS VERY IMPORTANT IN UNDERSTANDING THE MESSAGES THAT ARE CONVEYED BY PHOTOGRAPHY AND ILLUSTRATION...

...AND BY PAINTING, GRAPHIC DESIGN, SCULPTURE, ARCHITECTURE, VIDEO -- ANY MEDIA THAT WE ENGAGE WITH OUR EYES.

THIS IS THE LOGO FOR THE HUMAN RIGHTS CAMPAIGN, A GROUP THAT FIGHTS LAWS AGAINST GAY MARRIAGE.

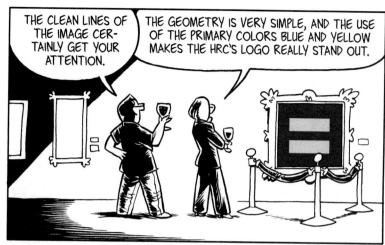

THE CLEAN LINES OF THE IMAGE CERTAINLY GET YOUR ATTENTION.

THE GEOMETRY IS VERY SIMPLE, AND THE USE OF THE PRIMARY COLORS BLUE AND YELLOW MAKES THE HRC'S LOGO REALLY STAND OUT.

IT USES **NEGATIVE SPACE** TO DRAW THE VIEWER'S EYES TO THE CHANNEL BETWEEN THE TWO RECTANGLES, WHICH CONNECTS THE SPACES ON EITHER SIDE.

THE IMAGE ALSO USES **SYMMETRY**.

TOP AND BOTTOM AND RIGHT AND LEFT MIRROR EACH OTHER.

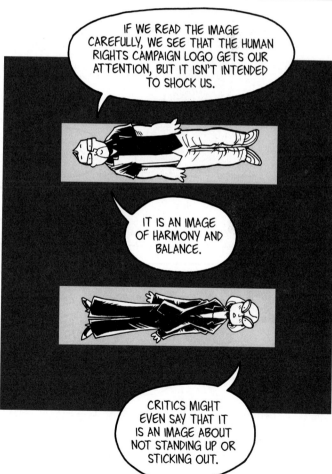

IF WE READ THE IMAGE CAREFULLY, WE SEE THAT THE HUMAN RIGHTS CAMPAIGN LOGO GETS OUR ATTENTION, BUT IT ISN'T INTENDED TO SHOCK US.

IT IS AN IMAGE OF HARMONY AND BALANCE.

CRITICS MIGHT EVEN SAY THAT IT IS AN IMAGE ABOUT NOT STANDING UP OR STICKING OUT.

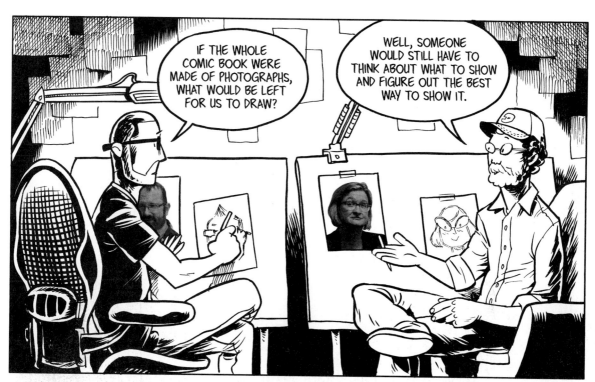

IF THE WHOLE COMIC BOOK WERE MADE OF PHOTOGRAPHS, WHAT WOULD BE LEFT FOR US TO DRAW?

WELL, SOMEONE WOULD STILL HAVE TO THINK ABOUT WHAT TO SHOW AND FIGURE OUT THE BEST WAY TO SHOW IT.

THAT'S TRUE.

THE BOOK AS A WHOLE WOULD STILL HAVE TO MAKE A GOOD VISUAL ARGUMENT.

CRUMPLE

SPEAKING OF VISUAL ARGUMENTS, WHY DO YOU ALWAYS DRAW SO MANY DIAGONAL LINES?

UH...

...I DON'T THINK THAT'S THE KIND OF ARGUMENT THEY MEAN.

BUT WHY DO YOU USE SO MANY DIAGONAL LINES?

Introduction

Why rhetoric? Why a COMIC BOOK?

Odio cuando mi madre insiste en hablar en vietnamita frente a la gente.

[I HATE IT WHEN MY MOTHER INSISTS ON SPEAKING IN VIETNAMESE IN FRONT OF PEOPLE.]

MY DAUGHTER IS VERY GOOD WITH LANGUAGES.

I CAN SEE THAT.

Yo no estaba coqueteando contigo. Yo sólo estaba siendo amable.

[I WASN'T FLIRTING WITH YOU. I WAS JUST BEING FRIENDLY.]

WHOOPS!

I NEVER THOUGHT I'D COME TO COLLEGE AND MY FIRST TEXTBOOK WOULD BE A **COMIC BOOK!**

I KNOW WHAT YOU MEAN.

I **LIKE** COMICS, BUT I DON'T THINK OF THEM AS **TEXTBOOKS.**

C'MON, IT'S ONLY THE FIRST DAY OF CLASS.

KEEP AN **OPEN MIND!**

MY MOM'S READING IT TOO!

SHE'S TAKING NIGHT CLASSES, AND HER TEACHER IS USING THE SAME BOOK!

I NEVER THOUGHT I'D BE GOING BACK TO SCHOOL SO LATE, BUT AT LEAST MY DAUGHTER AND I CAN STUDY TOGETHER!

BUT MY CLASS IS ACTUALLY **HARDER** THAN HERS.

WE'RE ALSO **CREATING** GRAPHIC NOVELS THAT TELL THE STORIES OF OUR OWN LIVES.

THEY'RE CALLED **MEMOIRS**, MOTHER.

GRAPHIC MEMOIRS.

MY SPANISH MAY NOT BE GREAT, BUT MY ENGLISH IS FINE.

I HOPE YOU DON'T TALK THIS WAY TO **YOUR** MOTHER.

PART OF WRITING A **GRAPHIC MEMOIR** IS HAVING TO DRAW **ONESELF!**

I'M A LITTLE **INTIMIDATED.**

IN MY WRITING CLASS, SOME OF THE STUDENTS ARE REALLY GREAT AT DRAWING!

BUT THERE ARE A LOT OF THINGS THAT THOSE STUDENTS **DON'T** KNOW HOW TO DO.

LIKE **PAY ATTENTION.**

SOME OF THEM HAVE MANNERS THAT ARE ALMOST AS BAD AS HERS.

COME ON, MOM. I'M SURE THAT THE OTHER STUDENTS AREN'T REALLY THAT BAD.

YOU SHOULD TRY TO MAKE FRIENDS.

I DON'T WANT TO TALK ABOUT OUR PERSONAL BUSINESS.

YOU SHOULDN'T BE EMBARRASSED, MOM.

AND BEING A GOOD ARTIST DOESN'T REALLY MATTER AS MUCH AS YOU THINK IT DOES.

IT SOUNDS LIKE THE PROJECT IS ABOUT TELLING A COMPELLING STORY AND MAKING AN INTERESTING VISUAL ARGUMENT.

LIKE IN MY LAB REPORT HERE, I HAVE TO USE THESE CHARTS AND GRAPHS TO CONVINCE THE TEACHER THAT I'VE DONE THE EXPERIMENT CORRECTLY.

CHARTS AND GRAPHS ARE ONE THING. BUT WHAT DO I DO WITH THIS PAGE SHOWING MY TIME IN THE REFUGEE CAMP ENGLISH CLASS?

...IT FEELS TOO **DENSE** OR SOMETHING.

ACTUALLY, IT'S REALLY INTERESTING TO SEE HOW MUCH INFORMATION YOU PACK INTO THE PAGE.

BUT WHAT IF YOU REALLY DEVELOPED THE CHARACTER OF YOUR TEACHER?

YOU COULD BREAK UP THIS FRAME INTO INDIVIDUAL FRAMES, AND WE WOULD KNOW THAT YOU WERE SHOWING DIFFERENT EPISODES IN TIME.

COMING UP IN THE NEXT EXCITING EPISODE OF **REFRAME**

"What does ARISTOTLE have to do with ME?"

[pg. 55]

DRAWING CONCLUSIONS

The following assignments ask you to try out the
concepts discussed in this introduction.

1 Think about your own writing
processes for various situations --
from formal (such as an academic
essay) to informal (such as
a comment on an online video).
Consider both individual work and
collaborations with others.

Map out what your processes look
like. What differences do you notice?
What prompts you to make changes
as you work through each process?

2 Watch a video of a person speaking to a live
or online audience (you might try TEDTalks to
find sources). Afterward, make notes on what
you remember most clearly; then watch the video
again, paying attention to what you see when the
most memorable information is presented.

What information does the speaker convey visually,
either with media accompanying the talk or with
body language? How well do the visuals and words
work together?

3 In the ReFrame for this chapter, Carol is working on her graphic memoir. Using both words and images, make a draft of what your own graphic memoir might look like.

What would you choose to emphasize? How would you make your central ideas and themes clear?

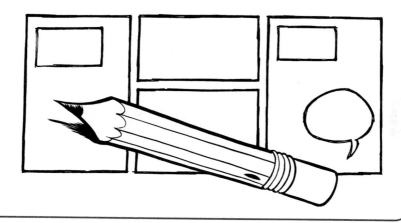

4 Comic artists often arrange panels to suggest different perceptions of time. Browse graphic novels or other comics to find creative depictions of the experience of passing time. Then create a storyboard for a short comic about an event that seemed to you to occur much more slowly or more quickly than you know it actually did.

Present your storyboard to others in your class and get feedback on how well your method works.

bedfordstmartins.com/understandingrhetoric

ISSUE 1
WHY RHETORIC?
ARISTOTLE LIVES!
In this issue...
PIECING TOGETHER A DEFINITION OF RHETORIC
Page 36
REANIMATING ANCIENT VIEWS OF RHETORIC
Page 39
SETTING RHETORICAL CONCEPTS LOOSE ON THE WORLD
Page 43
ETHOS
PATHOS

IS THAT A RHETORICAL QUESTION?!!

HMF.

SOME PEOPLE CALL A QUESTION **"RHETORICAL"** BECAUSE NO ANSWER IS ACTUALLY EXPECTED.

DO I LOOK **STUPID** TO YOU?

ACCORDING TO THEM, RHETORIC AND RHETORICAL ARE ALL ABOUT **SHUTTING DOWN** CONVERSATION AND DEBATE!

BUT I--⁙

ACTUALLY, THE ANCIENTS DEVELOPED THE CONCEPT OF **RHETORIC** TO **FACILITATE** DISCUSSION.

THEY THOUGHT THAT RHETORIC PROVIDED A SET OF SKILLS THAT HELPED PEOPLE FOREGROUND IDEAS --

-- DISCUSS AND DEBATE THEIR THOUGHTS WITH OTHERS --

-- AND POTENTIALLY REACH COMMON GOALS OR MAKE DIFFICULT DECISIONS.

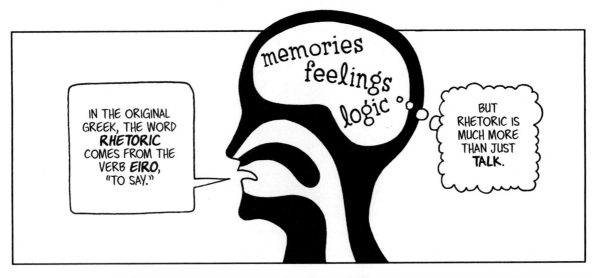

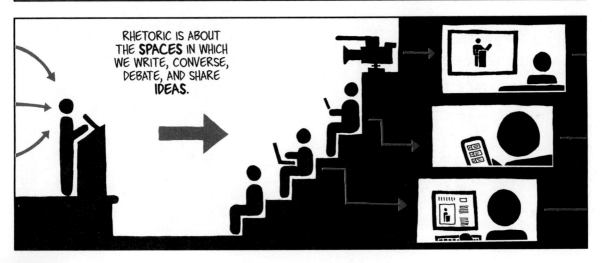

REANIMATING ANCIENT VIEWS OF RHETORIC

MANY COMMONLY HELD NEGATIVE IDEAS ABOUT RHETORIC CAN BE TRACED TO THE ANCIENT GREEK PHILOSOPHER **PLATO**.

HE BELIEVED THAT TEACHERS LIKE US WHO TAUGHT RHETORIC WERE INSTRUCTING THEIR STUDENTS TO DECEIVE OTHERS RATHER THAN TO BETTER THEMSELVES.

IF SERIOUS DISCUSSION IS LIKE GYMNASTICS, THEN RHETORIC IS LIKE **COSMETICS**.

RHETORIC IS INTENDED ONLY TO HIDE FLAWS, NOT ENCOURAGE SELF-IMPROVEMENT.

PLATO (427–347 BCE)
ANCIENT GREEK PHILOSOPHER, STUDENT OF SOCRATES, AND FOUNDER OF THE ATHENIAN ACADEMY, AN IMPORTANT EARLY SCHOOL OF THOUGHT.

AS FAR AS PLATO WAS CONCERNED, RHETORIC WAS AN EMPTY, UNWHOLESOME DISTRACTION THAT TOOK ATTENTION AWAY FROM IMPORTANT PHILOSOPHICAL AND CIVIC MATTERS.

INDULGING THE POPULATION'S APPETITE FOR RHETORIC IS AS BAD AS SELLING **PASTRIES** INSTEAD OF DISPENSING **MEDICINE**.

PLATO ALSO THOUGHT THAT VIVID MEDIA EXPERIENCES, SUCH AS ANCIENT GREEK TRAGEDIES THAT SHOWED EXPLICIT SEX AND VIOLENCE, WOULD HAVE A BAD INFLUENCE ON YOUNG PEOPLE.

ALL POETS AND PLAYWRIGHTS SHOULD BE **BANISHED!**

PLATO FELT THAT THE YOUNG SHOULD BE PROTECTED FROM AMBIGUOUS MORAL MESSAGES.

PRETENDING TO BE CRIMINALS CAUSES CHILDREN TO GROW UP TO BE CRIMINALS IN REAL LIFE. EVERYONE KNOWS THAT.

PLATO WASN'T JUST WORRIED ABOUT CHILDREN. HE BELIEVED THAT THE INVENTION OF WRITING IN THE ANCIENT WORLD ALLOWED ADULTS TO LIE ABOUT THE TRUTH, PRETEND TO BE SOMEONE THEY WERE NOT, OR FORGET THE PAST AND TRADITION.

JUST AS PEOPLE WORRY TODAY ABOUT MANY OF THE EFFECTS OF TECHNOLOGY ON WRITING, PLATO WORRIED ABOUT THE EFFECT OF WRITING ON OUR ABILITY TO SPEAK THE TRUTH.

THINGS WERE SURE A LOT BETTER BEFORE WE HAD **WRITING!**

PLATO'S STUDENT **ARISTOTLE** HAD A VERY DIFFERENT VIEW ABOUT WRITING AND RHETORIC.

ARISTOTLE WAS A PROPONENT OF THE USE OF RHETORIC TO PUT ACROSS A BROAD RANGE OF IDEAS.

ARISTOTLE (384–322 BCE)
ANCIENT GREEK PHILOSOPHER (AND STUDENT OF PLATO) WHOSE THINKING CONTRIBUTED MUCH TO THE DEVELOPMENT OF WESTERN EMPIRICAL AND SCIENTIFIC THOUGHT.

ARISTOTLE THOUGHT THAT PLAYS COULD SERVE AN **EDUCATIONAL** PURPOSE BY ENCOURAGING GREEK CITIZENS TO DEVELOP THEIR CAPACITIES FOR PITY AND FEAR.

BY SEEING THE CONSEQUENCES OF SEXUAL AND VIOLENT CRIMES THAT WERE COMMITTED BY ACTORS ON STAGE, SPECTATORS COULD LEARN **NOT** TO IMITATE BAD **ACTIONS**.

IN **THE ART OF RHETORIC,**

ETHOS IS THE CREDIBILITY THAT A SPEAKER OR WRITER BRINGS TO THE SUBJECT THAT HE OR SHE IS COMMUNICATING ABOUT.

WE TRUST CERTAIN KINDS OF PEOPLE MORE THAN OTHERS -- BECAUSE THEY HAVE EXPERTISE, OR BECAUSE THEY ARE WELL INFORMED ABOUT THE SUBJECT AT HAND.

PATHOS IS THE USE OF EMOTION IN DEBATE OR ARGUMENT.

APPEALS TO PATHOS SURROUND US, PARTICULARLY IN VISUAL ARGUMENTS SUCH AS ADVERTISEMENTS AND MANY ONLINE VIDEOS.

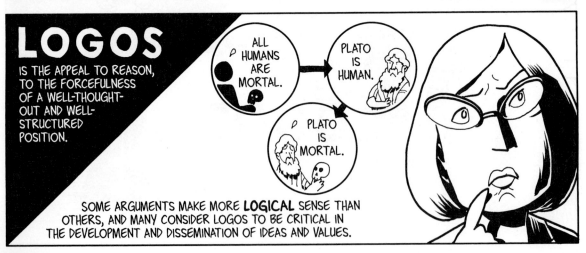

LOGOS IS THE APPEAL TO REASON, TO THE FORCEFULNESS OF A WELL-THOUGHT-OUT AND WELL-STRUCTURED POSITION.

SOME ARGUMENTS MAKE MORE **LOGICAL** SENSE THAN OTHERS, AND MANY CONSIDER LOGOS TO BE CRITICAL IN THE DEVELOPMENT AND DISSEMINATION OF IDEAS AND VALUES.

 WE GENERALLY DON'T THINK OF SOCIAL NETWORK PROFILES AS MAKING "LOGICAL ARGUMENTS," BUT IN A WAY, THEY **ARE** MAKING ARGUMENTS --

-- ARGUMENTS ABOUT WHO WE ARE, WHAT WE ARE INTERESTED IN, AND WHY SOMEONE MIGHT WANT TO "FRIEND" US.

 @JONATHAN: Are you trying to seem cool by having a social network homepage?

BUT RHETORIC ISN'T JUST ABOUT **SPACE**. IT IS ALSO ABOUT **TIME**.

BENDING TIME through KAIROS

ALL OF US HAVE HAD EXPERIENCES THAT WERE EMBARRASSING, INSULTING, HUMILIATING, OR DEMORALIZING.

OFTEN WE WISH THAT WE COULD HAVE TRAVELED BACK IN TIME TO SAY JUST THE RIGHT THING AT THAT PARTICULAR MOMENT.

WE MAY COME UP WITH THE PERFECT THING TO HAVE SAID MUCH LATER, BUT IT IS ALREADY TOO LATE.

I-I KNOW YOU ARE, BUT WHAT AM I...?

today: AUDITIONS 5-9 pm

DEBATES ABOUT DIFFICULT ISSUES ARE OFTEN TIME-SENSITIVE.

...VOTING TO REDUCE SPENDING ON UNIVERSITIES...

REELECT ME

BUT...

TUITION BILL

OFTEN, THERE IS A NARROW WINDOW WITHIN WHICH ONE CAN SPEAK OUT TO AFFECT AN ISSUE.

NO TUITION HIKES

FUND HIGHER EDUCATION

MORE TUITION HIKES

IN A LEGAL PROCEEDING, PARTICIPANTS ARE EXPECTED TO SPEAK ONLY AT CERTAIN TIMES.

...right to peaceably assemble...

...AND PRAISE OR BLAME FOR PEOPLE IN THE PUBLIC EYE MAY SWAY OPINIONS AT CRUCIAL MOMENTS.

MY CONGRESSMAN STANDS UP FOR STUDENTS. DOES YOURS?

Liz's Boyfriend is on the prowl.

Ladies like this

Plato: I... my bro, w... nd time f...t?

Aristotle: want to... tonigh...

Liz's Boyfriend
Relationship Status:
FINALLY SINGLE!

FOR EXAMPLE, USERS OF SOCIAL NETWORK SITES OFTEN ANNOUNCE CHANGES IN RELATIONSHIP STATUS...

...OFTEN BEFORE THEIR **PARTNERS** ARE INFORMED.

ON THE OTHER HAND, WAITING TOO **LONG** CAN DOOM YOUR COMMUNICATION EFFORTS.

HAPPY V-DAY! <3

KISS ME I'M IRISH

MARCH

SOMETIMES, HOWEVER, PEOPLE MANAGE TO SAY THE RIGHT THING AT JUST THE RIGHT MOMENT, AND THOSE PARTICULARLY **APT** WORDS ARE REMEMBERED FOR **CENTURIES**.

FAMOUS LAST WORDS -- SUCH AS NATHAN HALE'S

"I only regret that I have but one life to lose for my country."

-- ARE STILL QUOTED TODAY.

CICERO THOUGHT ABOUT THE "TEXTS" OF RHETORIC VERY BROADLY AND REALIZED THAT SPEECHES AND WRITING ARE NOT THE ONLY WAYS PEOPLE COMMUNICATE.

THE ROMANS DEVELOPED AN ELABORATE SYSTEM OF LAWS AND PUBLIC ENGINEERING PROJECTS TO REGULATE AN INCREASINGLY COMPLEX SOCIETY.

THESE **RES PUBLICA**, OR "PUBLIC THINGS," ARE WORTH CONSIDERING AS RHETORICAL ACTS AND SPACES.

AS ARCHEOLOGISTS KNOW, EVEN GOVERNMENT BUILDINGS AND TRIUMPHAL ARCHES CONVEYED MESSAGES TO CITIZENS IN THE ANCIENT ROMAN WORLD AND PRESENTED IMPLICIT ARGUMENTS ABOUT AUTHORITY, PARTICIPATION, AND SHARED VALUES.

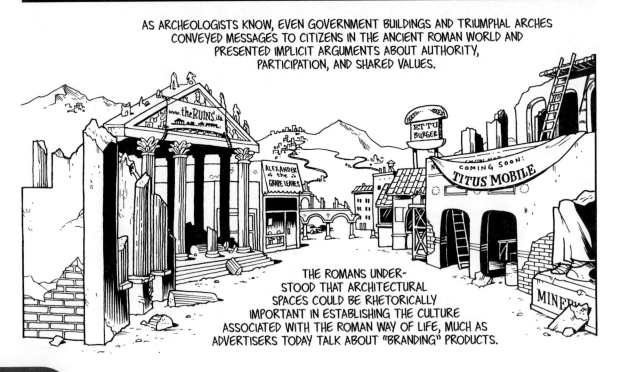

THE ROMANS UNDERSTOOD THAT ARCHITECTURAL SPACES COULD BE RHETORICALLY IMPORTANT IN ESTABLISHING THE CULTURE ASSOCIATED WITH THE ROMAN WAY OF LIFE, MUCH AS ADVERTISERS TODAY TALK ABOUT "BRANDING" PRODUCTS.

CICERO ALSO TAUGHT HIS STUDENTS TO IMAGINE

THEY WOULD REMEMBER

EACH PART

OF THE SPEECH

THE PARTS OF THEIR SPEECHES AS ROOMS IN A BUILDING,

SO THAT AS THEY WALKED THROUGH THE BUILDING

IN THEIR MINDS,

IN ORDER.

WHAT ARE YOU DOING?

OMM...

I'M TRYING TO REMEMBER WHAT WE TALKED ABOUT IN THIS CHAPTER.

WELL, EVEN THOUGH MEMORIZATION IS NO LONGER AS IMPORTANT AS IT ONCE WAS, SOME THINGS ABOUT RHETORIC REMAIN THE SAME.

...AND BOY ARE MY ARMS TIRED! [HOW 'BOUT LUNCH?]

EVEN AFTER THOUSANDS OF YEARS!

TO: l.losh@univ.edu
SUBJECT: HEY

Hey Mrs. Losh: I'm super busy on Friday. Please let me know if we do anything important. TTYL.

Luis

REMEMBER WHEN WE TALKED ABOUT **ETHOS** IN CLASS?

ethos

YOU DON'T MAKE YOURSELF SOUND LIKE SOMEONE WHO HAS A GOOD REASON TO BE EXCUSED. IN FACT, YOU SOUND LIKE KIND OF A JERK.

AND REMEMBER, YOU'RE ASKING FOR A **FAVOR** FROM YOUR PROFESSOR. BUT YOUR EMAIL SOUNDS LIKE YOU'RE ADDRESSING ANOTHER **STUDENT**, NOT YOUR TEACHER.

THAT COULD BE A BIG MISTAKE.

PART DOW

YOU NEED AN APPEAL TO **PATHOS** -- TO MAKE HER FEEL A CERTAIN WAY, RIGHT? BUT YOUR SUPER-CASUAL APPROACH MIGHT EARN YOU A RE-ACTION YOU DON'T WANT.

AND DON'T FORGET **LOGOS** -- ORGANIZ-ING WHAT YOU WANT TO SAY INTO A COMPELLING ARGUMENT OR STORY.

REASONS APOLOGIES EXCUSES PLANS EXPLANATIONS

KAIROS PATHOS ETHOS

WOW, YOU **WERE** REALLY PAYING ATTENTION IN CLASS!

BUT I SEE WHAT YOU MEAN. LET ME TRY MAKING IT A BIT MORE LIKE A FORMAL LETTER.

TO: l.losh@univ.edu
SUBJECT: Upcoming Absence

Dear Dr. Losh,

My older brother is on active duty in the military and is being deployed this month. My extended family will have his going-away party on Friday. I'd very much like to be there, given the circumstances. May I be excused from class? I'll be happy to make up any work, and I will ask my classmates for notes.

Sincerely,

Luis

TO: luis@univ.edu
SUBJECT: RE: Upcoming Absence

Dear Luis,

Thanks for the heads-up. We'll be starting brainstorming and process work on your first assignment, an analysis of the design of a print advertisement for an on-campus organization, service, or cause.

You should analyze the rhetorical strategies of the advertisement by commenting on its logos, pathos, ethos, and kairos. You should study details in the wording, images, typography, organization, and visual design on the page. Let me know if you have any questions, and I'll see you in class on Monday.

Best,
Liz

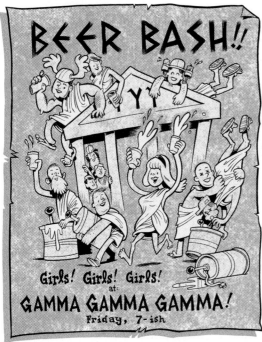

I SEE WHAT YOU MEAN -- THEY ARE TOTALLY DIFFERENT.

WE CAN START WITH THESE QUESTIONS:

Calling all PROSPECTIVE PLEDGES!

JOIN US AT AN **INFORMATIONAL LUNCHEON** TO

★ Get a HEAD START on building your RÉSUMÉ!

★ Learn new SKILLS!

★ NETWORK with potential COLLEAGUES and EMPLOYERS!

SPONSORED BY
BETA BETA BETA

Monday, November 2nd
11 am - 1 pm
[No shorts or jeans, please!]

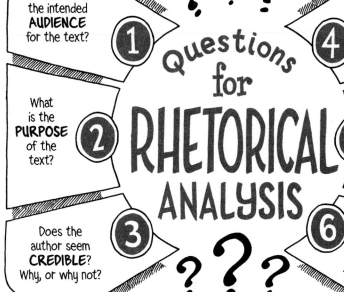

Questions for RHETORICAL ANALYSIS

1. Who is the intended AUDIENCE for the text?

2. What is the PURPOSE of the text?

3. Does the author seem CREDIBLE? Why, or why not?

4. What is your gut REACTION to the text? What EMOTIONS does it evoke?

5. How are the elements arranged or ORGANIZED? Why? Does the arrangement seem LOGICAL?

6. When and where was the text WRITTEN? Was it timely given this context? Why, or why not?

QUICK REVIEW:

ETHOS
The credibility that a speaker/ writer brings to a subject.

PATHOS
Use of emotion in debate/ argument.

LOGOS
Appeal to reason, to the forcefulness of a well-thought-out and well-argued position.

Calling all **PROSPECTIVE PLEDGES!**

JOIN US AT AN **INFORMATIONAL LUNCHEON** TO

 Get a HEAD START on building your RÉSUMÉ!

 Learn new SKILLS!

 NETWORK with potential COLLEAGUES and EMPLOYERS!

SPONSORED BY

BETA BETA BETA

Monday, November 2nd
11 am – 1 pm

[*No shorts or Jeans, Please!*]

COMING UP IN THE NEXT EXCITING EPISODE OF **REFRAME**

" How do I **READ** this?"

[pg. 103]

DRAWING CONCLUSIONS

The following assignments ask you to practice thinking about the rhetorical strategies of **ETHOS**, **LOGOS**, **PATHOS**, and **KAIROS**.

 Write an analysis of your social network page or the page of someone famous, such as a politician or celebrity. Make your analysis a *rhetorical* analysis by focusing on the use of logos, pathos, and ethos on the page.

Consider also the particular components of the Web page that allow a user to craft an identity online. What kinds of strategies help you and others compose with greater rhetorical effectiveness? Where and how on the page could its creator make more effective rhetorical choices?

 Jot down some ideas about the rhetorical characteristics of informal and formal writing. In what ways are they similar? In what key ways are they different? Now, pick a kind of formal writing that you either are working on now or have encountered in the past.

Think about how a consideration of logos, ethos, pathos, and kairos could help you compose the piece better, or how it might have helped you improve a piece you've already written.

3

If you have a social network profile page, consider what you already know about the two meanings of kairos. What kinds of postings are intended to be appreciated during a period of only a day or even a few hours? What kinds of postings are intended to be seen for years to come?

Write an essay in which you describe your experience of kairos while using social network sites, and make some recommendations for your peers. Perhaps your essay can take the form of a "how to" guide.

4

This chapter incorporates many illustrations of ancient rhetoricians and philosophers. Find another image of Aristotle, Plato, or Cicero online -- perhaps from the ancient world or the Renaissance -- and compare it to the drawings in this book.

What do you think each image suggests about the person, and why do you think the image's creator wanted to give that impression?

bedfordstmartins.com/understandingrhetoric

ISSUE 2
STRATEGIC READING
In this issue...
INVESTIGATING TEXTS AND ANALYZING MEANING
Page 68
PUTTING THE PIECES TOGETHER WITH SYNTHESIS
Page 80
USING READING STRATEGIES
Page 90
IMAGINING IDEAL READERS
Page 94

WHEN WE READ WE OFTEN SEE PICTURES IN OUR **MINDS**.

FOR EXAMPLE...

...TAKE THIS PASSAGE FROM AN **EARLY VERSION** OF THE AUTOBIOGRAPHY OF FREDERICK DOUGLASS, WHO DESCRIBES HIS EXPERIENCES AS AN **ESCAPED SLAVE**.

WE'VE BROKEN UP THE WORDS SO THAT INDIVIDUAL PASSAGES ARE ILLUSTRATED, AS THEY MIGHT BE IN A READER'S IMAGINATION, TO MAKE SOME POINTS ABOUT A PROCESS KNOWN AS

CRITICAL READING!

"I have been frequently asked how I felt when I found myself in a free State. I have never been able to answer the question with any satisfaction to myself."

"It was a moment of the highest excitement I ever experienced."

WHAT'S THE DIFFERENCE IN EFFECT BETWEEN **"HIGHEST EXCITEMENT"** AND **"GREATEST EXCITEMENT"**?

I THINK **"HIGHEST"** IS A LOT MORE **VIVID** -- "HIGH" EVOKES AN ELEVATION IN STATUS, IN THIS CASE FROM **SLAVE** TO **FREE CITIZEN.**

"I suppose I felt as one may imagine the unarmed mariner to feel when he is rescued by a friendly man-of-war from the pursuit of a pirate."

"But the loneliness overcame me. There I was in the midst of thousands, and yet a perfect stranger; without home and without friends, in the midst of thousands of my own brethren—children of a common Father...

INTERESTING THAT HE SAYS "BRETHREN" AND "A COMMON **FATHER**" INSTEAD OF "BROTHERS AND SISTERS" OR "A COMMON **MOTHER**"?

IT COULD JUST BE A **GUY** THING.

...LET'S COME BACK TO THAT LATER.

"...and yet I dared not to unfold to any one of them my sad condition. I was afraid to speak to any one for fear of speaking to the wrong one...

"...and thereby falling into the hands of money-loving kidnappers, whose business it was to lie in wait for the panting fugitive...

"...as the ferocious beasts of the forest lie in wait for their prey."

"The motto which I adopted when I started from slavery was this--'Trust no man!'"

"I saw in every white man an enemy...

"...and in almost every colored man cause for distrust.

"It was a most painful situation;...

"...and, to understand it, one must needs experience it, or imagine himself in similar circumstances."

"Let him be a fugitive slave in a strange land--

--a land given up to be the hunting-ground for slaveholders--

"whose inhabitants are legalized kidnappers--

--where he is every moment subjected to the terrible liability of being seized upon by his fellowmen,"

COMPREHENSIVE CRITICAL READING MAY REQUIRE YOU TO SEARCH FOR SPECIALIZED CONCEPTS IN A WRITER'S WORK....

...BUT THE GENERAL STRATEGIES THAT FOLLOW CAN SERVE YOU WELL WHEN YOU READ ANY TEXT.

SOMETIMES YOU ARE CONSIDERING IF THE LANGUAGE IS **EXTREME**.

HYPERBOLE!!! VS. understatement.

SOMETIMES YOU ARE LOOKING FOR INFORMATION THAT THE AUTHOR HAS **OMITTED**.

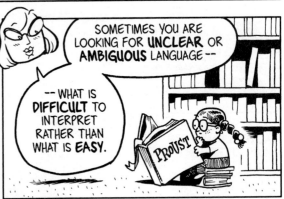

SOMETIMES YOU ARE LOOKING FOR **UNCLEAR** OR **AMBIGUOUS** LANGUAGE --

-- WHAT IS **DIFFICULT** TO INTERPRET RATHER THAN WHAT IS **EASY**.

READING IN THIS WAY...

...IS CALLED **ANALYSIS**.

YOU CAN DO THE **SAME THING** WITH THIS TEXT. SUPPOSE YOU TOOK ALL OF DOUGLASS'S IMAGES OF **WILD ANIMALS** -- AND **WILD MEN** -- FROM THE PASSAGE PRESENTED EARLIER AND **SEPARATED THEM OUT** FROM THE REST OF THE TEXT.

FOCUSING ON THIS KIND OF LANGUAGE WITH **ANIMAL IMAGERY** MIGHT HELP YOU UNDERSTAND THE PREDATORY NATURE OF **SLAVERY**, AND HOW THE INSTITUTION OF SLAVERY TREATS HUMANS LIKE **ANIMALS**.

ABOLITIONIST IMAGERY

OR YOU COULD LOCATE ALL THE TIMES THAT DOUGLASS TALKS ABOUT HOW HE FELT BUT CREATES SOME **SEPARATION** FROM THE EVENTS THAT HE IS RECORDING.

York, I said I felt like d. I suppose I felt as one ma imagine the unarmed mariner to feel when he is rescued by a friendly man-of-war from the pursuit

OFTEN HE DOES THIS BY ADDING MORE **EMOTIONAL DISTANCE** WITH EXTRA VERBS ABOUT **"SAYING"** OR **"SUPPOSING"** IN RELATION TO HIS FEELINGS.

WRITERS SOMETIMES LEAVE **IMPLICIT MESSAGES** IN THEIR TEXTS -- FROM THE LATIN IMPLICARE, MEANING "TO ENFOLD."

WRITE WRITE

FOR EXAMPLE, WHEN DOUGLASS CREATES **SEPARATION** FROM HIMSELF AND HIS DESCRIPTION OF SLAVERY, HE IS TRYING TO ESTABLISH HIMSELF AS AN **OBJECTIVE OBSERVER** OF SLAVERY, NOT JUST A **VICTIM** OF IT.

STUFF STUFF

FREDERICK DOUGLASS

THE **IMPLICIT MESSAGE** HERE IS THAT WE CAN **TRUST** DOUGLASS.

ANOTHER WAY TO THINK ABOUT CRITICAL READING IS TO THINK ABOUT IT AS **EXPLICATION**.

to **EXPLICATE** is to **UNFOLD**

THE WORD **EXPLICATION** COMES FROM THE LATIN *EXPLICARE*, WHICH MEANS "TO UNFOLD."

EXPLICATION IS THE PROCESS OF **REVEALING** OR **UNCOVERING** IDEAS OR BELIEFS BURIED IN THE TEXT.

DOUGLASS'S PREJUDICES ABOUT CITIES

DOUGLASS'S IDEAS ABOUT THE NATURAL WORLD

DOUGLASS'S ATTITUDES ABOUT AFRICA

THESE IDEAS ARE NOT OBVIOUS; THEY ARE ONLY **SUGGESTED**, PERHAPS **INDIRECTLY**, BY THE TEXT.

FOR INSTANCE, DOUGLASS COMPARES POTENTIAL KIDNAPPERS TO "HIDEOUS CROCODILES."

DOUGLASS WAS WELL AWARE THAT MANY CONSIDERED SLAVES TO BE **ANIMALS**. IN A NICE **REVERSAL**, HIS METAPHOR OF THE CROCODILE IMPLIES THAT **SLAVEHOLDERS** REALLY ARE THE BEASTS.

IF YOU REMEMBER WHAT WE LEARNED ABOUT **PATHOS, LOGOS, ETHOS,** AND **KAIROS** YOU CAN SEE THAT THOSE ARE ALSO AT WORK HERE.

OBVIOUSLY, DOUGLASS IS TRYING TO STIR HIS AUDIENCE'S **EMOTIONS,** BY USING LANGUAGE THAT SUGGESTS THAT **PITY AND FEAR** ARE APPROPRIATE RESPONSES TO HIS TEXT.

THE IMAGES THAT WE MIGHT REMEMBER BEST ARE THE IMAGES OF **EXOTIC SCENES, WILD ANIMALS,** AND **SAVAGE PEOPLES,** WHICH ARE DESIGNED TO EXCITE OUR **EMOTIONS.**

TRUST NO MAN

PATHOS

WE CAN ALSO SEE THAT DOUGLASS IS MAKING A NUMBER OF **LOGICAL COMPARISONS** OF SEEMINGLY UNLIKE THINGS.

HE DESCRIBES SLAVE TRADERS AS **BEASTLY**...

...AND HE NOTES THAT ESCAPED SLAVES MIGHT FIND NEW YORK CITY TO BE AS MUCH A PART OF THE SYSTEM OF TERROR AS THE SLAVE-HOLDING **SOUTH**.

HE IS WRITING ABOUT A SUPPOSEDLY CIVILIZED COUNTRY, **AMERICA**, NOT A PLACE LIKE AFRICA, WHICH MANY IN THE UNITED STATES IMAGINED TO BE **VIOLENT** AND **WILD**.

LOGOS

THERE ARE ALSO MANY POINTS IN THIS PASSAGE WHERE DOUGLASS IS CONCERNED WITH HIS **AUTHORITY**, AS A SPEAKER AND WRITER.

HE WAS "**FREQUENTLY ASKED**" HOW HE FELT ABOUT BEING FREE IN NEW YORK, WHICH IMPLIES THAT HIS OPINION WAS SOUGHT BY **MANY**.

ETHOS

SYNTHESIS INVOLVES MAKING MEANING FROM MULTIPLE SOURCES.

FOR EXAMPLE, THERE WASN'T JUST ONE EDITION OF DOUGLASS'S BOOK.

...THERE WERE MANY!

AND, AS DOUGLASS TOLD HIS LIFE STORY, IT GOT A LOT LONGER.

THE FIRST VERSION OF HIS BOOK WAS JUST 124 PAGES.

BY THE END OF HIS LIFE, WHEN HE WROTE THE LIFE AND TIMES OF FREDERICK DOUGLASS, HIS AUTOBIOGRAPHY HAD GROWN TO OVER 700 PAGES.

THAT'S A LOT OF MATERIAL TO SYNTHESIZE!

THAT'S NOT ALL.

THERE WERE ALSO ILLUSTRATIONS IN DOUGLASS'S BOOKS THAT WE MIGHT WANT TO ANALYZE AND THEN SYNTHESIZE.

AFTER ALL, ACCORDING TO **EYEWITNESSES**, THE REAL-LIFE DOUGLASS WAS ABOUT **SIX FEET TALL** AND VERY PHYSICALLY **IMPOSING**.

DOUGLASS WAS DEEPLY CONCERNED ABOUT THE WAY ILLUSTRATIONS IN BOOKS DEPICTED HIM.

BUT WE NEED TO DO SOME MORE **SYNTHESIS** TO PROVE THAT THESIS.

HERE'S A CLUE.

IN 1849 DOUGLASS PRAISED AN **ILLUSTRATED BOOK** ABOUT FAMOUS AFRICAN AMERICANS.

IN THE REVIEW, HE ALSO **RIDICULED** AN ILLUSTRATION OF HIMSELF, , WHICH HE SAID HAD A

"much more kindly and amiable expression, than is generally thought to characterize the face of a fugitive slave."

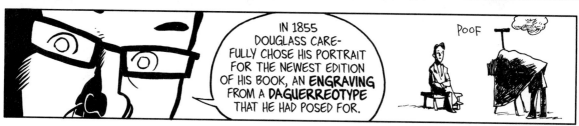

IN 1855 DOUGLASS CAREFULLY CHOSE HIS PORTRAIT FOR THE NEWEST EDITION OF HIS BOOK, AN **ENGRAVING** FROM A **DAGUERREOTYPE** THAT HE HAD POSED FOR.

POOF

BY **ASSEMBLING INFORMATION FROM MULTIPLE SOURCES**, WE CAN REALLY SAY SOMETHING INTERESTING ABOUT A WORK AND HOW TO READ IT CRITICALLY --

-- EVEN ONE THAT PEOPLE THINK THAT THEY ALREADY KNOW **WELL**, LIKE DOUGLASS'S AUTOBIOGRAPHY.

WITH SOMEONE LIKE DOUGLASS THERE MIGHT BE A LOT OF MATERIAL TO SYNTHESIZE.

LET'S GO BACK TO THE **ORIGINAL BOOK** AND ITS 124 PAGES.

YOU CAN DO SYNTHESIS THERE, TOO.

SOMETIMES A SINGLE BOOK IS ACTUALLY MADE UP OF **MANY KINDS OF SOURCES**.

LOOKING AT THE **SOURCES** THAT A WRITER USES MAY GIVE US CLUES THAT LEAD TO **ADDITIONAL INFORMATION**.

THEN WE NEED TO BRING ALL THAT MATERIAL TOGETHER AND SUPPORT A **THESIS** ABOUT WHAT IT ALL ADDS UP TO MEAN.

BIBLICAL PASSAGES

PHILOSOPHICAL SNIPPETS

LETTERS

PREFACES

POEMS

MAIPS

ILLUSTRATIONS

BOOKS FROM OUR **OWN** TIME OFTEN CONTAIN A LOT OF DIFFERENT KINDS OF TEXTS **TOO**.

A **CELEBRITY BIOGRAPHY** MIGHT INCLUDE **NEWSPAPER STORIES** OR EVEN **BEAUTY TIPS** AND RECIP --!

?!?

SNATCH

I CAN'T TAKE YOU **ANYWHERE**.

WHEN DOUGLASS'S BOOK INITIALLY APPEARED, SOME DOUBTED ITS **AUTHENTICITY**.

THEY THOUGHT THAT FUGITIVE SLAVES **EXAGGERATED** THEIR STORIES OR THAT AFRICAN AMERICANS WEREN'T **LITERATE** ENOUGH TO WRITE ANYTHING DOWN.

PROMINENT MEN ATTESTED TO DOUGLASS'S **LITERACY** AND **HONEST CHARACTER** IN LETTERS INCLUDED AT THE FRONT OF HIS BOOK.

THEY WEREN'T **CO-AUTHORS** OF HIS BOOK, BUT THEY WERE **FELLOW WRITERS** IN IT.

THESE PEOPLE THOUGHT THAT ACCOUNTS FROM FUGITIVE SLAVES MUST REALLY BE THE **FICTIONS** OF WHITE **ABOLITIONISTS**.

DOES THIS MEAN THAT I NEED TO FIND OUT MORE ABOUT **WILLIAM LLOYD GARRISON** AND **WENDELL PHILLIPS**?

THIS IS **WAY TOO MUCH TO SYNTHESIZE** FOR A THREE- TO FIVE-PAGE **PAPER**!

WHEN DOES IT **STOP**?

THE SECRET TO DOING **SYNTHESIS** IS FOCUSING ON **MANAGEABLE** TASKS.

HERE, LET ME GIVE YOU ONE MORE EXAMPLE.

NOT **ANOTHER** EXAMPLE!

RELAX. THIS ONE HAS **PICTURES**.

OKAY.

I LIKE THE EXAMPLES WITH PICTURES.

OFTEN WHEN DOING **SYNTHESIS**, IT HELPS TO THINK OF THINGS AS **SETS**.

LET'S TAKE THIS SET OF **EIGHTEEN ILLUSTRATIONS** FROM THE LAST EDITION OF DOUGLASS'S AUTO-BIOGRAPHY.

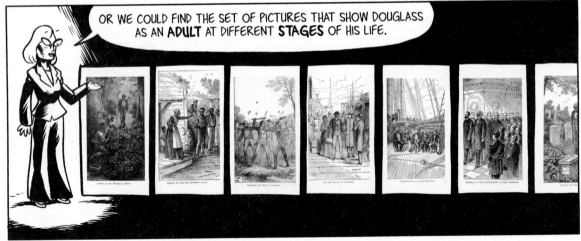

OR WE COULD FIND THE SET OF IMAGES THAT SHOW **WHITE ABOLITIONIST CELEBRITIES.**

BUT **HARRIET BEECHER STOWE** IS ALREADY IN THE "**WOMEN**" SET.

WHEN YOU SORT IMAGES INTO **CATEGORIES,** THE SAME PIECE OF **EVIDENCE** COULD BE SYNTHESIZED WITH MORE THAN ONE POSSIBLE **GROUP.**

YOU CAN DO THE SAME THING WITH **PASSAGES** FROM WRITTEN TEXTS THAT WE JUST DID WITH THESE **ILLUSTRATIONS.**

SOME PEOPLE USE **INDEX CARDS** WITH **QUOTATIONS** FOR THIS PURPOSE.

GREAT!

I'LL WRITE THE **TITLE** OF DOUGLASS'S BOOK ON AN **INDEX CARD.**

LIFE AND TIMES OF FREDERICK DOUGLASS, WRITTEN BY HIMSELF. HIS EARLY LIFE AS A SLAVE, HIS ESCAPE FROM BONDAGE, AND HIS COMPLETE HISTORY TO THE PRESENT TIME, INCLUDING HIS CONNECTION WITH THE ANTI-SLAVERY MOVEMENT; HIS LABORS IN GREAT BRITAIN AS WELL AS IN HIS OWN COUNTRY; HIS EXPERIENCE OF...

THE UNDERGROUND RAILROAD; HIS RELATIONS WITH JOHN BROWN AND THE HARPERS FERRY RAID; HIS RECRUITING THE 54TH AND 55TH MASS. COLORED REGIMENT; HIS INTERVIEWS WITH PRESIDENTS LINCOLN AND JOHNSON; HIS APPOINTMENT BY GEN. GRANT TO ACCOMPANY THE SANTO DOMINGO COMMISSION—ALSO TO A SEAT IN THE COUNCIL AND HIS APPOINTMENT AS...

HIS APPOINTMENT TO BE RECORDER OF DEEDS IN WASHINGTON BY PRESIDENT J.A. GARFIELD; WITH MANY OTHER INTERESTING AND IMPORTANT EVENTS OF HIS MOST EVENTFUL LIFE; WITH AN INTRODUCTION BY MR. GEORGE L. RUFFIN, OF BOSTON. HARTFORD, CONN: PARK PUBLISHING CO., CROSWELL & J.S. GOODMAN, SAN FRAN...

OR MAYBE **NOT.**

AS I SAID, THE SECRET TO DOING **SYNTHESIS** IS FOCUSING ON MANAGEABLE **TASKS.**

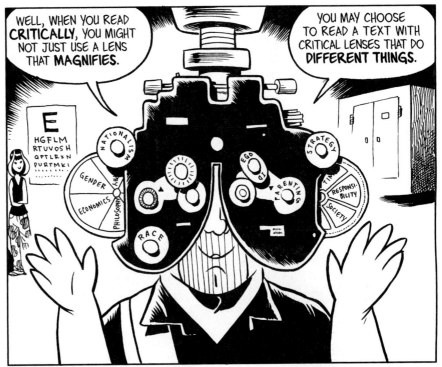

YOU CAN READ A BOOK AS THOUGH YOU ARE READING IT **THROUGH** ANOTHER BOOK--

--**APPLYING** THE IDEAS, PHILOSOPHY, OR METHODS OF ANALYSIS FROM ONE TEXT TO ANOTHER.

SOMETIMES YOU READ A TEXT **SIDE BY SIDE** WITH ANOTHER TEXT, NOTING THE SIMILARITIES AND DIFFERENCES BETWEEN THE TWO.

WRITING TEACHERS CALL THIS "**COMPARISON** AND **CONTRAST**."

COMPARISON HAS BEEN PART OF RHETORICAL INSTRUCTION SINCE ANCIENT TIMES. IT'S AN IMPORTANT KIND OF **SYNTHESIS** IN CRITICAL READING.

IN **HUMANITIES** CLASSES, ESSAY EXAMINATIONS USUALLY ASK **COMPARISON** AND **CONTRAST** QUESTIONS, BUT THEY SOMETIMES POSE **APPLICATION** QUESTIONS AS WELL.

Compare the text of Douglass's narrative to Olaudah Equiano's slave narrative, which was written many years earlier. Both men were abolitionist speakers who urged the passage of antislavery legislation in the United States and in Great Britain respectively, but they had very different rhetorical techniques. How do they describe captivity and injustice? How do they describe their literacy and public speaking?

Apply W. E. B. DuBois's theory of "double consciousness" to the text of Frederick Douglass's Narrative. In what ways does Douglass seem to experience double consciousness as he interacts with both white and black participants in his story?

WHEN I **COMPARE AND CONTRAST** TWO TEXTS...

...I START BY MAKING LISTS OF HOW THEY'RE ALIKE AND HOW THEY'RE DIFFERENT.

WITH **APPLICATION** QUESTIONS...

...I CAN APPLY THE THEORETICAL TEXTS I'M READING TO NEW **SITUATIONS**.

FOR INSTANCE, I MIGHT APPLY IDEAS FROM **PLATO** AND **ARISTOTLE** TO A GRAPHIC NOVEL I READ FOR A LIT CLASS.

93

IMAGING IDEAL READERS

THERE'S **ANOTHER** KIND OF CREATIVE EXERCISE THAT INVOLVES CRITICAL READING.

IT INVOLVES THINKING ABOUT **IDEAL READERS** WHEN EXAMINING A TEXT.

DOUGLASS IS MAKING A VERY **SPECIFIC** RHETORICAL APPEAL TO THE READER TO IDENTIFY WITH HIS PLIGHT IN **NEW YORK**...

...EVEN THOUGH THE SITUATION OF A **FUGITIVE SLAVE** MAY SEEM FAR REMOVED FROM THE CONCERNS OF HIS PRIVILEGED WHITE **AUDIENCES**.

HE IS **ALSO** URGING HIS READERS TO BE **SELF-CRITICAL** AND TO CONSIDER INJUSTICE DONE TO OTHERS THAT IS CLOSER TO HOME THAN THEY MIGHT **REALIZE**.

"GOOD"

"BAD"

TO HELP PERSUADE OTHERS, WRITERS OFTEN IMAGINE AN **IDEAL READER**.

AS HE WROTE, DOUGLASS PROBABLY CONSIDERED HOW A PERSON FROM HIS OWN **TIME** BUT OF A **DIFFERENT RACE** MIGHT READ HIS BOOK.

"I say, let him place himself in my situation--without home or friends--without money or credit--wanting shelter, and no one to give it--wanting bread, and no money to buy it,

"--and at the same time let him feel that he is pursued by merciless men-hunters..."

"--perfectly helpless both as to the means of defence and means of escape,

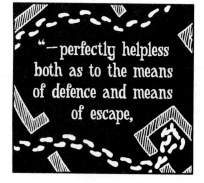

"--in the midst of plenty, yet suffering the terrible gnawings of hunger,--in the midst of houses, yet having no home,

"--among fellow-men, yet feeling as if in the midst of wild beasts, whose greediness to swallow up the trembling and half-famished fugitive is only equalled by that with which the monsters of the deep swallow up the helpless fish upon which they subsist,"

YOUR IDEAL READER FOR THE ESSAYS THAT YOU WRITE IN **COLLEGE** MAY BE VERY MUCH LIKE **YOURSELF**, PARTICULARLY IF YOU ARE PREPARING SOMETHING TO BE READ BY A GROUP OF **PEERS**.

OR YOUR IDEAL READER MIGHT BE MORE OF AN **EXPERT** ON THE SUBJECT TO WHOM YOU WILL WANT TO DEMONSTRATE YOUR **MASTERY** OF THE COURSE MATERIAL.

PEER

YOU

PROFESSOR

PUBLIC

IT IS ALWAYS HELPFUL TO ENVISION A READER **APPROPRIATE** TO A GIVEN PURPOSE AND TO THE PARTICULAR RHETORICAL OCCASION OR **KAIROS**.

YOU MAY THINK YOU DON'T KNOW ENOUGH ABOUT **FREDERICK DOUGLASS** OR THE **PRE-CIVIL WAR PERIOD** IN U.S. HISTORY TO UNDERSTAND WHAT DOUGLASS WANTED READERS TO KNOW.

BUT ANY READER WHO PAYS ATTENTION AND USES SMART READING STRATEGIES CAN LEARN TO EXPLICATE A TEXT AND UNCOVER MEANINGS.

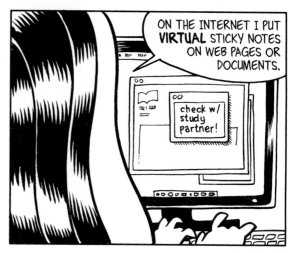

ba-DOOP!

Reading on the Internet offers opportunities to interact with texts and writers.

Many Web sites offer links to free social bookmarking tools that let you share what you are reading with friends.

thanks! =-)

I'M **CONFUSED** HERE.

WHEN I'M CONFUSED, SOMETIMES I LOOK THINGS UP ON THE WEB.

BUT IT IS TRUE THAT IF YOU ARE GOING TO USE THE MATERIAL FROM THE WEB IN A **WRITING ASSIGNMENT**, YOU SHOULD CHECK TO SEE IF IT COMES FROM A RELIABLE **SOURCE*** --

-- A SOURCE WRITTEN BY **RECOGNIZED EXPERTS** WITH THE AUTHORITY TO SPEAK OR WRITE ABOUT AN ISSUE.

* For more on research, see CHAPTER 5.

AND YOU'LL NEED TO EVALUATE THE SOURCE NO MATTER **WHERE** YOU FIND IT.

DON'T BE AFRAID TO TALK TO YOUR INSTRUCTORS AS WELL.

the PROF

YOU CAN **ALSO** ASK OTHER PEOPLE FOR HELP WITH A DIFFICULT PASSAGE.

TRADITIONALLY, READING HAS BEEN A SOCIAL PROCESS IN WHICH WE SHARE OUR EXPERIENCES OF READING WITH **OTHERS**.

IN THE EIGHTEENTH AND NINE- TEENTH **CENTURIES**, PEOPLE OFTEN SHARED **BOOKS** AND **NEWSPAPERS** WITH FRIENDS, AND FAMILIES READ **OUT LOUD** TOGETHER EACH NIGHT.

SOME **LITERACY SPECIALISTS** SAY THAT EVEN TODAY READING ALOUD ISN'T JUST FOR **KIDS**.

THE MORE THAT STUDENTS UNDERSTAND THAT READING IS A **PUBLIC** AND **SOCIAL ACTIVITY**, THE MORE THEY **IMPROVE**.

SOMETIMES I NEED TO GO OVER A PAGE MORE THAN **ONCE**.

GOOD READERS AREN'T NECESSARILY **FAST** READERS.

AND YOU MIGHT SEE SOMETHING IN A TEXT THAT ANOTHER STUDENT **DOESN'T** SEE.

THANKS, I THINK THAT --

WOW!

SEE?

REFRAME with Luis & Cindy

How do I READ this?

103

DO YOU HAVE TO ANALYZE THE **WORDS** OR THE **IMAGES** OR **BOTH**?

THAT'S THE TRICKY PART, LUIS. ANALYZING **IMAGES** IS TOUGHER THAN I THOUGHT. BUT I FEEL PRETTY CONFIDENT TALKING ABOUT THE **WRITTEN** TEXT.

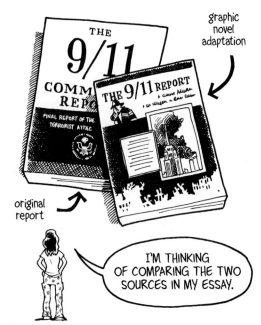

graphic novel adaptation

original report

AFTER ALL, THE INFORMATION COMES STRAIGHT FROM THE **ACTUAL REPORT** OF THE 9/11 COMMISSION.

SOME OF THE LANGUAGE IS EVEN THE SAME, **WORD-FOR-WORD**, LIKE THE TITLES OF THE CHAPTERS.

I'M THINKING OF COMPARING THE TWO SOURCES IN MY ESSAY.

EVEN BEFORE THEY TURNED IT INTO A COMIC, PARTS OF THE ORIGINAL REPORT READ MORE LIKE A **THRILLER** THAN A DRY LEGAL DOCUMENT.

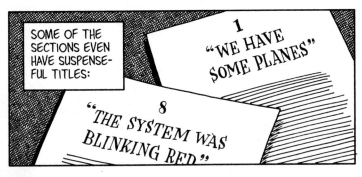

SOME OF THE SECTIONS EVEN HAVE SUSPENSE-FUL TITLES:

1 "WE HAVE SOME PLANES"

8 "THE SYSTEM WAS BLINKING RED"

I GUESS THE WRITERS OF THE **GOVERNMENT REPORT** REALLY WANTED TO GRAB PEOPLE'S ATTENTION BY DRAMATICALLY SETTING THE **SCENE**.

YEAH, THE **ORIGINAL REPORT** BEGINS WITH A DESCRIPTIVE OPENING...

THE 9/11

"TUESDAY, SEPTEMBER 11, 2001, dawned temperate and nearly cloudless in the eastern United States."

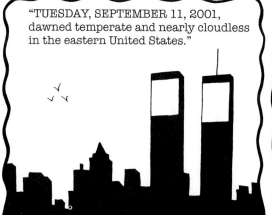

"Millions of men and women readied themselves for work."

"Some made their way to the Twin Towers, the signature structures of the World Trade Center complex in New York City."

"Others went to Arlington, Virginia, to the Pentagon."

"Across the Potomac River, the United States Congress was back in session."

"At the other end of Pennsylvania Avenue, people began to line up for a White House Tour."

"In Sarasota, Florida, President George W. Bush went for an early morning run."

THAT'S A LOT LIKE THE SECTION I JUST READ ABOUT "STRATEGIC READING." FREDERICK DOUGLASS ALSO USED VERBAL PICTURES TO MAKE HIS ARGUMENT MORE ENGAGING AND CONVINCING.

BUT READING CRITICALLY MEANS MORE THAN JUST IMAGINING YOURSELF IN THE SCENE.

YOU HAVE TO ANALYZE THE CHOICE OF INDIVIDUAL ELEMENTS IN THE TEXT AND HOW THEY FIT TOGETHER IN WAYS THAT MIGHT NOT BE IMMEDIATELY OBVIOUS.

THAT SOUNDS LIKE MUCH LESS OF A THRILLER.

WELL, THERE'S STILL SOMETHING SATISFYING ABOUT ASSEMBLING ALL THOSE CLUES. I MEAN, LOOK BACK AT THAT OPENING.

THE FIRST SENTENCE IS UP IN THE CLOUDLESS SKY.

BUT THE SECOND TAKES PLACE DOWN ON THE GROUND AT THE HUMAN LEVEL.

"TUESDAY, SEPTEMBER 11, 2001, dawned temperate and nearly cloudless in the eastern United States."

"Some made their way to the Twin Towers, the signature structures of the World Trade Center complex in New York City."

"Across the Potomac River, the United States Congress was back in session."

"At the other end of Pennsylvania Avenue, people began to line up for a White House Tour."

"in Sarasota, Florida, President George W. Bush went for an early morning run."

THE THIRD SENTENCE IS ABOUT THE PRIVATE SECTOR, AND THE FOURTH IS ABOUT THE MILITARY, ALTHOUGH THEY BOTH DISCUSS DAILY COMMUTERS ON THE MOVE.

AND THE REST OF THE OPENING IS ABOUT THE PEOPLE WHO MIGHT BE ULTIMATELY RESPONSIBLE FOR PREVENTING ANOTHER TERRORIST ATTACK: THE LEGISLATIVE AND EXECUTIVE BRANCHES OF GOVERNMENT.

IN THE **GRAPHIC NOVEL**, THE FIRST SENTENCE FOCUSES DIRECTLY ON THE PLANES.

"BEFORE 8 O'CLOCK ON TUESDAY, SEPTEMBER 11, 2001, A PLEASANT AND CLOUDLESS MORNING IN BOSTON, TWO PLANES, BOTH BOEING 767S, WERE ABOUT TO TAKE OFF FROM LOGAN AIRPORT."

SO WHEN YOU LOOK CLOSELY AT THE **LANGUAGE** AND THE **LOGIC** OF A PASSAGE, YOU CAN ACTUALLY SEE **IMPLICIT ARGUMENTS** THERE.

RIGHT. BUT YOU HAVE TO **EXPLICATE** THEM.

OR **UNFOLD** THEM.

UNFOLD

READING THE **WORDS** IS EASY. I DON'T KNOW WHAT TO SAY ABOUT READING THE **PICTURES**.

?

KNOCK KNOCK!

UH...

...LUIS, I'LL HAVE TO CALL YOU BACK.

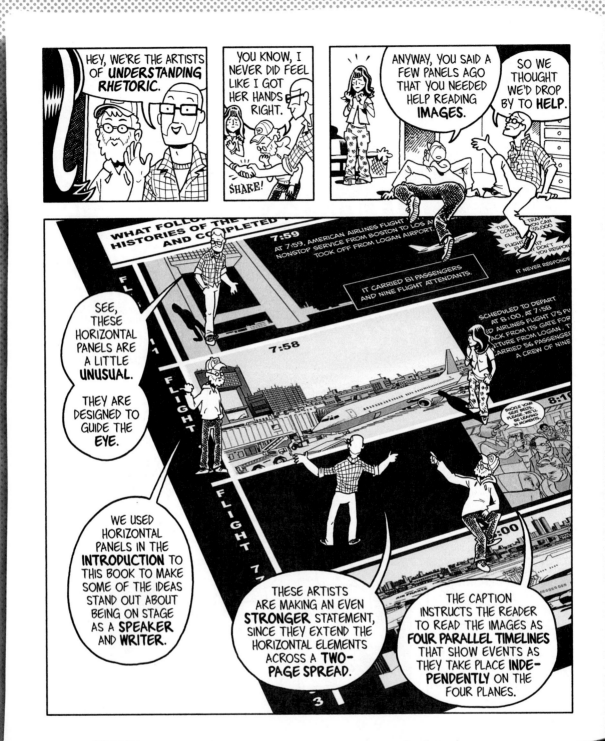

WHAT'S INTERESTING IS HOW MUCH **BLACK** THE COMIC INCLUDES.

THEY EMPHASIZE THE SERIOUS, SOBER QUALITY OF THE EVENT BY USING THE COLOR BLACK, A COLOR TRADITIONALLY ASSOCIATED WITH **MOURNING** IN OUR COUNTRY.

WE'RE FINALLY OFF, LADIES AND GENTLEMEN.

THANKS FOR THE **TIPS!**

BLACK ALSO FOCUSES THE READER'S ATTENTION ON HOW MANY THINGS THAT HAPPENED IN THE HIJACKINGS ARE STILL **UNKNOWN**, BECAUSE INVESTIGATORS ARE STILL "IN THE DARK" ABOUT EXACTLY WHAT TOOK **PLACE**.

Beep Beep Beep Beep

HEY, LUIS, I HAVE SOME-THING TO **SHOW** YOU...

...AND THEN I HAVE TO GET BACK TO **READING**.

COMING UP IN THE NEXT EXCITING EPISODE OF **REFRAME**

"What's my IDENTITY?"

[pg. 135]

DRAWING CONCLUSIONS

The activities below ask you to focus on the rhetorical dimensions of texts and visuals you might write about.

1 Choose one print text and one nonprint text that you are currently reading. Consider all of the ways you "notate" what you read, either in writing or in your head. Do you make real notes? Use stickies? Use digital stickies? If you primarily use "mental stickies," what kinds of questions do you ask about what you read?

Write down some questions you might ask, or notes you might make, about the texts you have chosen.

2 Consider how you might use some terms from Chapter 1 -- logos, ethos, pathos, and kairos -- to engage in active reading. Pick a work you are reading for a class and make a note of the following: the subject, how the text builds logos, how the writer establishes ethos, how the text demonstrates a use of pathos, and how the writer shows an awareness of kairos.

What do you discover? How might attending to these rhetorical dimensions improve your ability to read -- and summarize -- a text?

3 Choose a text that you might be called upon to analyze, such as a journal article, a work of art, or a video or film. Make a list of all of the questions you have about it, as well as all of the points that you find interesting.

Next, make a list of quotations, still images, characteristics of the work, or other information that has popped out at you during your reading of the text.

Now group these pieces according to criteria that make sense to you, as Liz does with the images from Frederick Douglass's *Narrative* on pp. 87-89. Consider the questions you listed in light of your arrangement of pieces from the text. Rearrange questions and textual evidence as needed. What new insights emerge for you from this process?

4 Think about the book you're reading right now -- *Understanding Rhetoric.* Look back at the discussion on pp. 83-84 of Frederick Douglass's interest in controlling the way he appeared in images in print. Why do you think that this book uses Douglass as an example? What evidence do you find that indicates that the writers and illustrators of this book thought carefully about the images it includes? What choices might you have made differently?

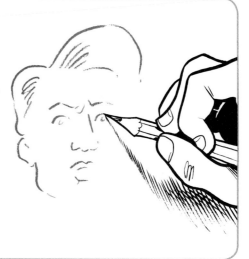

bedfordstmartins.com/understandingrhetoric

WRITING IDENTITIES

In this issue...

PHONE ★

117

A LOT OF PEOPLE TREAT PROFESSIONAL CLOTHING AS A KIND OF **ARMOR**.

IT GIVES THEM **AUTHORITY** AND MAKES THEM FEEL LESS **VULNERABLE**.

LIKEWISE, T-SHIRTS OFTEN MAKE CLEAR **RHETORICAL STATEMENTS**.

RUSTLE RUSTLE

FOR EXAMPLE, WEARING A T-SHIRT FROM A *STAR TREK* CONVENTION MIGHT SHOW THAT SOMEONE IS A BIG FAN.

LIVE LONG & PROSPER

THIS ONE IS FROM A VIDEO-GAME CONFERENCE, WHERE I GAVE A TALK ABOUT EDUCATIONAL GAMES.

GDC

SO ONE T-SHIRT IS ABOUT EXPRESSING YOUR ROLE AS A FAN, AND THE OTHER IS ABOUT YOUR ROLE AS AN ESTABLISHED EXPERT.

HERE'S A DRESS THAT I WORE WHEN I WAS A SUNDAY SCHOOL TEACHER.

MY STUDENTS EXPECTED ME TO BE FORMAL AND RESPECTABLE.

AND HERE ARE EXERCISE CLOTHES THAT I WEAR TO GYM CLASS WHEN I KNOW NOBODY'S LOOKING AT ME.

SOUNDS LIKE YOU HAVE A LOT OF DIFFERENT SOCIAL ROLES.

IN SOME ROLES YOU'RE A TEACHER, AND IN SOME YOU'RE A STUDENT.

SO YOU ALSO HAVE DIFFERENT LEVELS OF AUTHORITY.

127

YIKES!

A STATEMENT THAT OUTRAGEOUS WON'T PERSUADE **ANYONE** -- EVEN IF THE SENTIMENT BEHIND IT IS A VALID ONE.

HE NEEDS TO DIAL IT **DOWN**.

I KNOW! AN ATTACK LIKE THAT CAN CHANGE THE WAY AN AUDIENCE PERCEIVES THE ARGUMENT -- AND THE PERSON MAKING IT.

BUT IT'S ALSO POSSIBLE TO DIAL IT DOWN **TOO** FAR....

DOOP.

IT'S JUST MY OPINION, BUT SUPERCONGLOMERATE MIGHT POSSIBLY THINK ABOUT REEXAMINING ITS POLICIES ON GROUP HEALTH INSURANCE....

MAYBE.

SEE WHAT HAPPENS WHEN YOUR COMMUNICATION LACKS SPECIFICS AND ANY SENSE OF URGENCY?

ZZZ ZZZ

ALL OF US SUPERHEROES PUT OUR-SELVES AT RISK EVERY DAY -- AND THAT'S WHY PRIVATE INSURERS THINK WE'RE A BAD RISK.

WE SHOULDN'T HAVE TO RISK BANKRUPTCY TO KEEP FIGHTING EVILDOERS JUST BECAUSE WE'RE PART-TIMERS.

I SAVED THE MAYOR FROM A GIANT TARANTULA!

HOW OFTEN WILL I BE ABLE TO REPEAT SUCH FEATS IF I CAN'T AFFORD TREATMENT FOR MY INJURIES?

HEY, YOU'RE GOOD!

AWAKEN!

STRIKING A FORCEFUL YET MEASURED TONE ENCOURAGES YOUR AUDIENCE TO TAKE YOU SERIOUSLY.

YOU SOUND LIKE A REASONABLE PERSON WHO HAS A STAKE IN THE ARGUMENT.

YOUR **TONE** SHOULD ENGAGE YOUR AUDIENCE IN A WAY THAT WILL INVITE THEM TO FEEL RECEPTIVE TO YOUR MESSAGE.

AND YOUR **VOICE** -- YOUR IDENTITY AS A WRITER -- SHOULD PROJECT THE APPROPRIATE KIND OF AUTHORITY AND AGENCY.

RECORDING BOOTH

EXACTLY!

I ALWAYS NEED TO THINK ABOUT THE AUDIENCE I'M TRYING TO REACH IN MY RHETORICAL SITUATION -- AND MAKE SURE I ADJUST MY TONE AND VOICE TO GET THE EFFECT I WANT.

AHEM.

"INCLUDING ME AND MY FELLOW PART-TIME SUPERHEROES IN THE SUPERCONGLOMERATE GROUP INSURANCE PLAN IS THE RIGHT THING TO DO -- AND IN THE LONG RUN WILL BE MORE COST-EFFECTIVE THAN HAVING TO RECRUIT NEW SUPERHEROES TO REPLACE THOSE WHO CAN'T AFFORD TO KEEP WORKING FOR THE COMPANY."

REFRAME
with Luis & Cindy

What's my IDENTITY?

As an engineering major, I don't know that much about English literature, but I do think Shakespeare is pretty cool.

This sounds like a great résumé builder for me, and I'd love to get out of the house for the summer and make new friends. I'm a hard worker and a fast learner, so I'm sure that you won't be sorry if you choose me for this internship.

HMM...

Before coming to Campus University, Luis acted in a number of high school and community theater productions, including *Love's Labour's Lost*, *The Cherry Orchard*, and *Porgy and Bess*. He is the recipient of an Aimful Theatre Scholarship and is currently developing an experimental staging of *Twelfth Night* to be performed in the Northside Dining Hall.

A FEW HOURS LATER...

SORRY I HAD TO RUN.

THAT'S OKAY. HAVING YOUR BIO AS A MODEL WAS A HUGE HELP.

CHECK IT OUT!

Before coming to Campus University, Cindy was a professional actor. Her work in the film *Emma*, based on Jane Austen's novel, has been seen all over the world. She is the recipient of a Truong Family Theatre Scholarship. She will soon be making her debut at the local community arts complex.

OK, YOU SEEM TO BE MISREPRESENTING YOURSELF JUST A TINY BIT.

HOW CAN YOU SAY YOU WERE A PROFESSIONAL ACTOR SEEN ALL OVER THE WORLD? I DON'T REMEMBER YOU IN EMMA.

FOR MY HIGH SCHOOL ENGLISH CLASS, WE MADE A VIDEO OF A SCENE FROM EMMA. I PLAYED A MAID.

MY TEACHER REIMBURSED ME FOR MY COSTUME, SO I WAS KIND OF A PAID PERFORMER.

WE POSTED THE VIDEO ONLINE, SO PEOPLE IN OTHER COUNTRIES MIGHT HAVE SEEN IT.

As a founder of Gang of Geeks, a group of engineering students and actors devoted to making funny videos about surviving the first year as an engineering student, I've learned a lot about how to organize and plan an entertaining performance, give audiences a rewarding experience, and use social media creatively to promote our work. We've also involved local high school kids to encourage them to explore the creative aspects of math and engineering and to make college look like fun. As an intern in the Shakespeare Festival, I would bring fresh ideas about community outreach and a youthful sensibility to our productions, while also using my practical skills to help with inventory, accounting, and other offstage matters.

COMING UP IN THE NEXT EXCITING EPISODE OF **REFRAME**

"The OFFICE Hour!"

[pg. 171]

DRAWING CONCLUSIONS

The following assignments ask you to
think about creating effective arguments.

1 This chapter mentions Barbara Ehrenreich's
Nickel and Dimed, a book about the struggles
of the working poor that relies on the author's
experience of getting by on minimum-wage jobs.

What personal experiences have you had that
connect you to an idea or a subject that interests
you? How can you use your experiences to explore
that subject in a piece of writing? Draft a proposal
for a writing project in a genre of your choosing
(perhaps a Web essay or a newspaper editorial)
that uses your firsthand experience to enhance the
discussion of your topic.

2 Keep notes for a week about how you
interact with others through various
online sites. How do you represent
yourself -- in filling out required or
requested information, in uploading
content, and in interacting with others?

Write a short autoethnography -- a brief
narrative describing your own use of the
sites -- that analyzes your experiences
and discusses how you use different
identities in different rhetorical situations.

3

Look at pp. 127-28 of this chapter, in which extreme and bland tones are represented both verbally and visually. Choose a short text, such as an email or online posting, that you have written in the past month with a particular audience in mind.

Who is the audience? What tone do you take in your writing? Turn your original text into an audience-appropriate media text (perhaps a comic, collage, poster, or video) that uses visuals or other nonverbal means to help convey tone.

4

Many students feel anxiety about public speaking and presenting their ideas in front of large groups of people. What is the largest audience that you have ever had to address? How did you prepare for your presentation?

Looking back, what worked well, and what should you have done differently? How did the composition of the audience affect how you felt about your performance?

bedfordstmartins.com/understandingrhetoric

ARGUMENT
BEYOND PRO AND CON

SETTING THE SCENE FOR ARGUABLE ASSERTIONS

JUST LIKE IN THE ERA OF CLASSICAL RHETORIC, SPEAKERS ARE ALWAYS POINTING OUT HOW CIRCUMSTANCES **HAVE** CHANGED...

...**ARE** CHANGING...

...OR ARE **LIKELY** TO CHANGE.

AND THESE CHANGES MIGHT BE FOR THE WORSE OR FOR THE **BETTER**...

...AND THEY MIGHT BE GRADUAL "EVOLUTIONS" OR DRAMATIC "REVOLUTIONS"!

EXCUSE ME!

HEY, IF YOU REALLY WANT TO TALK ABOUT ARGUMENT, MAYBE YOU NEED A **TALK SHOW HOST!**

WHO INVITED **YOU** HERE?

THIS IS A PRIVATE CONVERSATION!

THIS DOESN'T LOOK LIKE A VERY **PRIVATE** CONVERSATION TO **ME.**

UNDERSTANDING RHETORIC
A Graphic Guide to WRITING

UH... RIGHT.

I GUESS WE **ARE** CHARACTERS IN A **BOOK.**

OKAY THEN...

K-CHONK!

A GOOD **ARGUMENT** IS ACTUALLY A LOT LIKE A GOOD **CONVERSATION.**

IT'S IMPORTANT TO REPRESENT **MORE** THAN ONE SIDE.

WHA--!

HUH?

GOOD POINT! IN A WAY, TALK SHOWS STAGE DEBATES AS CONVERSATIONS AMONG SEVERAL DIFFERENT PARTICIPANTS.

149

≥WHEW!≤ GUESTS ON TALK SHOWS SOMETIMES INSIST THAT ONLY **THEIR** SIDE CAN BE RIGHT, AND THE OTHER SIDE IS NECESSARILY **WRONG,** AND THEY NEVER CONCEDE **ANYTHING** TO THEIR OPPONENTS.

CON

PLEASE, MA'AM -- A GOOD ARGUMENT HAS TO GET BEYOND PRO AND CON DEBATES BETWEEN OVERSIMPLIFIED **OPPOSITES!**

RRGH! SIR!

COMPLEX CONVERSATIONS AREN'T JUST ABOUT **RIGHT** AND **WRONG!**

KICK!

POINT ACCUSINGLY!

No! No!! YES! PRO

IN THE DEBATE ABOUT **IMMIGRATION,** FOR INSTANCE, PARTICIPANTS ARE ACTUALLY ARGUING ABOUT THEIR VALUES AND THE DIFFERENT VISIONS THEY HAVE FOR THE COUNTRY.

VIEWED THAT WAY, THE DEBATE ABOUT IMMIGRATION ISN'T JUST ABOUT WHETHER TO LET IMMIGRANTS IN OR NOT. IT'S ALSO ABOUT HOW WE WANT TO DEFINE WHAT AMERICA IS.

MAYFLOWER

NO

CON

KICK 'em OUT!

YES

PRO

LET TH

THINKING ABOUT WHAT'S REALLY AT STAKE IN ANY GIVEN DEBATE REVEALS THE ARGUMENT'S **ASSERTIONS,** OR THE PARTICULAR CLAIMS BEING MADE.

A STATEMENT IS **ARGUABLE** IF IT REPRESENTS A POSITION WITH WHICH A REASON-ABLE PERSON COULD DISAGREE.

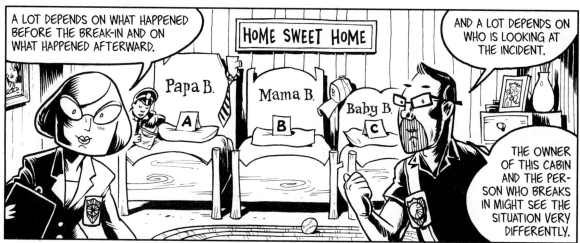

ZOOMING IN ON CLAIMS AND EVIDENCE

AN ARGUMENT NEEDS **GROUNDS** OR **EVIDENCE** FROM WHICH WE DEVELOP A POSITION.

WE CAME BACK FROM A WALK AND FOUND OUR FRONT DOOR STANDING **WIDE OPEN.**

MY PORRIDGE AND MY HUSBAND'S HAD CLEARLY BEEN TAMPERED WITH. YOU COULD EVEN SEE THE SPOON MARKS.

AND BABY BEAR'S HAD BEEN EATEN ALL UP.

IT WAS ALL GONE!!

HOW CAN A YOUNG BEAR GROW UP TO BE BIG AND STRONG WITHOUT ANY PORRIDGE?

HERE'S THE BEGINNING OF AN ARGUMENT BASED ON **EVIDENCE** --

-- THE BEARS ARE EXPLAINING:

1. **WHAT** happened,

2. **HOW** it happened,

3. **WHO** was affected, and

4. **WHY** it's a problem.

EMBEDDED IN ALL OF THOSE "QUESTION WORDS" IS A COMPLEX SET OF:

WHAT Facts

HOW Circumstances

WHO Relationships

WHY Reasons

...THESE CAN BE CRITICAL PARTS OF GOOD ARGUMENTS BASED ON EVIDENCE.

NOW -- WHAT IN THE **WORLD**?

POLICE

AHEM.

EVIDENCE CAN COME FROM COMPARING ONE CASE TO ANOTHER...

...AND FROM EXPERTS WHO CAN PROVIDE INFORMED **OPINIONS**.

THIS YOUNG WOMAN...

...WAS SUFFERING FROM **MALNOURISHMENT** AND **SLEEP DEPRIVATION**...

...THAT RENDERED HER INCAPABLE OF KNOWING RIGHT FROM WRONG.

ARGUMENTS IN COURT FOLLOW HIGHLY SPECIALIZED RULES...

...THAT DETERMINE WHAT EVIDENCE CAN BE INCLUDED, THE ORDER OF THE PRESENTATION...

BANG BANG ORDER!

LIZ!

...AND EVEN WHICH INFORMATION THE AUDIENCE -- THE JURORS -- CAN CONSIDER.

BOOT!

Y'KNOW, THEY WERE PROBABLY GOING TO HAVE A **CHEESE PLATE** OR SOMETHING IN THE JURY ROOM...

GIVE IT A **REST**, WILL YOU?

WHEN YOU TRY TO MAKE A PERSUASIVE ARGUMENT FOR COLLEGE OR FOR WORK, YOU MIGHT NOT USE THE KINDS OF CLAIMS AND EVIDENCE THAT A LAWYER WOULD CHOOSE.

YOU'LL NEED TO THINK ABOUT WHAT EVIDENCE WILL WORK IN THE CONTEXT OF **YOUR** ARGUMENT...

...AND HOW YOU CAN ORGANIZE AND PRESENT YOUR ARGUMENT MOST EFFECTIVELY.

IN CLASSROOMS AS IN COURTROOMS, ARGUMENTS ARE BUILT FROM THE GROUND UP--

EVIDENCE IS GATHERED, AND THEN LARGER CONCLUSIONS MAY BE DRAWN FROM IT.

SOMETIMES PRELIMINARY ARGUMENTS NEED TO BE REVISED...

CONCL-USIONS

EXTRAP-OLATION

EXAM-PLE   EXAM-PLE

ANALYSIS

EVIDENCE

BASE CLAIMS

GASP!

...AS...MORE EVIDENCE IS GATHERED...

The increasing generational differences between immigrants from Japan, the Issei, and the American-born second generation, the Nisei, had divided Japanese Americans even prior to the outbreak of World War II, and this division grew more apparent in the camps in which many Japanese Americans were interned during the war years. Nisei Gene Sogioka noted during his internment, "It's not just the age gap.... There are two different cultures in the camp: the Nisei, and the Issei"(qtd. in Gesenseway 153). The disparity between ancient Japan and modernized America was embodied and displayed by the contrasting values, ideologies, and lifestyles of the Issei and Nisei. The Issei often insisted that Japanese be spoken throughout the camp; the Nisei, however, symbolized the idealistic quest for the "American Dream" and willingly conformed to U.S. customs (Dusselier 195). The camp structure intensified the estrangement between Issei parents and their Nisei children because the young people were no longer economically dependent on their parents; by taking away any rights to income or social status, the U.S. government had usurped the position of primary caregiver, and the structure of the Japanese American family unit neared disintegration (Ziegler 136; Dusselier 194). Due to the inability of each group to understand or accept the other's behaviors, an antagonistic relationship developed. Ted Matsuda, interned at Jerome, Arkansas, describes in his evacuation diary the frequent problems with stealing occurring in the camp (21). In his June 15 entry, he bitterly recounts, "Issei are quick to blame every fault on the Nisei" (21). Through the disunion between the Issei and Nisei, the cultural identification term "Japanese American" became fragmented by the opposing sides of its two competing ethnicities.

Adapted from an essay by Marissa Osato

SO-- --LET'S TALK ABOUT HOW THE PARTS OF AN ARGUMENT WORK AS A WHOLE.

B-BUT-- BUT MY SANDWICH--

WELCOME BACK!

YOU'RE JUST IN TIME FOR THE NEXT QUESTION!

PRO CON

WHEN I WAS IN HIGH SCHOOL, THEY TAUGHT US TO WRITE **FIVE-PARAGRAPH** ESSAYS:

AN **INTRODUCTION.**

THREE EXAMPLES TO PROVE THE POINT.

AND A **CONCLUSION** THAT RESTATES THE INTRODUCTION.

WELL, MOST WRITING YOU DO AFTER HIGH SCHOOL WON'T FOLLOW SUCH A SIMPLE FORMULA.

RIGHT-- --PEOPLE DON'T USUALLY WRITE THAT WAY WHEN THEY HAVE SOMETHING TO SAY AND AN AUDIENCE TO SAY IT TO.

ALL RIGHT --

-- THEN LET'S LOOK AT AN EXAMPLE OF THE KIND OF ARGUMENT THAT A COLLEGE INSTRUCTOR MIGHT FACE.

OKAY...

RECENTLY, JONATHAN AND I HAVE BEEN DEBATING WHETHER OR NOT GRADES SHOULD BE RELEASED TO PARENTS OF COLLEGE-AGED STUDENTS.

I AM LEANING TOWARD **YES**.

AND I'M LEANING TOWARD **NO**.

SEEMS LIKE A PRETTY STRAIGHTFORWARD DEBATE ON TODAY'S

"PRO and CON!"

ER...

...MR. HOST...

...NOT **EXACTLY**. I MEAN, IT MIGHT LOOK LIKE THAT ON THE SURFACE, BUT SITUATIONS ARE SELDOM SO SIMPLE.

IT'S TRUE THAT WE ARE STARTING WITH DIFFERENT ASSERTIONS...

...BUT I THINK THERE ARE STILL SOME THINGS THAT WE AGREE ON.

AND MAYBE WE'LL REACH A CONCLUSION THAT IS SOMEWHERE BETWEEN OUR TWO STARTING POSITIONS.

LET'S HEAR FROM OUR AUDIENCE.

YES, MA'AM -- YOUR QUESTION?

IN FACT, THE LAWS CREATED BY THE FAMILY EDUCATIONAL RIGHTS AND PRIVACY ACT [FERPA] REQUIRE THAT STUDENTS WAIVE IN WRITING THEIR RIGHT TO PRIVACY IF THEY'D LIKE THEIR PARENTS TO KNOW ABOUT THEIR GRADES.

CINDY'S GRADES

SO THE **LAW** IS ACTUALLY ON THE SIDE OF STUDENTS' PRIVACY.

WE CAN ARGUE WHETHER THAT LAW IS GOOD OR NOT.

the LAW

IS IT USEFUL AND HELPFUL FOR STUDENTS' SUCCESS IN COLLEGE?

WE COULD ALSO ASK ABOUT **CAUSE AND EFFECT** -- HOW MIGHT THE FERPA GUIDELINES LEAD TO GREATER STUDENT RESPONSIBILITY?

CAUSE & EFFECT

OR **NOT**?

ARGUING ALONG THESE LINES MIGHT ALSO ALLOW US TO ADDRESS THE QUESTION OF THE VALUES REPRE-SENTED BY THE GUIDELINES.

VALUES

FURTHERMORE, WHILE WE SEEM TO BE STARTING FROM DIFFERENT POSITIONS IN THIS ARGUMENT...

...WE SHOULD ALSO CONSIDER WHAT BOTH POSITIONS HAVE IN COMMON.

YES!

BOTH ASSERTIONS ARE FRAMED BY THE DESIRE TO HAVE STUDENTS **SUCCEED** IN COLLEGE!

I DON'T HAVE MUCH OF A DRAFT YET FOR MY RESPONSE AND COUNTERARGUMENT ASSIGNMENT.

THAT'S OKAY.

YOU CAN COME TO OFFICE HOURS JUST TO HAVE A CONVERSATION ABOUT HOW TO GET STARTED.

SO...

...I READ THE BOOK BY ANYA KAMENETZ THAT YOU ASSIGNED, ABOUT REFORMING THE U.S. COLLEGE SYSTEM...

DIY U

ME TOO!

CAN WE TALK ABOUT IT TOGETHER?

SURE!

OKAY, SO...

...WHAT DID YOU THINK OF *DIY U*?

TO BE HONEST, MOSTLY I AGREE WITH THE AUTHOR.

I WORRY ABOUT THE RISING COST OF EDUCATION.

AND I WORRY ABOUT THE QUALITY OF EDUCATION I'M GETTING IN COLLEGE.

ch-CHING! ch-CHING

$138 per class hour!!

$ $ $ $

ch-ch ing

I USED TO THINK IT WAS ALL ABOUT GETTING GOOD GRADES, BUT NOW THAT TUITION FOR COLLEGE KEEPS GOING UP...

GRADES A

BILL $

ABSOLUTELY! STUDENTS ARE RIGHT TO WORRY ABOUT GETTING GOOD GRADES AND KEEPING THEIR PARENTS HAPPY.

BUT A LOT OF THEM ALSO CARE ABOUT THE BIG PICTURE AND THEIR FINANCIAL FUTURES.

173

I WISH IT WERE THAT SIMPLE!

THINK OF WHAT WE TALKED ABOUT IN CLASS.

EXPLAINING RISING TUITION RATES IS LIKE EXPLAINING WHY DUTCH PEOPLE HAVE GOTTEN TALLER.

YOU NEED TO GRAPPLE WITH CONFLICTING THEORIES.

COLLEGE IS PART OF THE "AMERICAN DREAM," SO POTENTIAL STUDENTS CREATE A HUGE DEMAND FOR HIGHER EDUCATION.

HIGH DEMAND DRIVES UP PRICES, ESPECIALLY WHEN SO MANY STUDENTS WANT TO GO TO A SELECTIVE FOUR-YEAR SCHOOL.

THAT DEMAND IS STOKED BY MARKETERS WHO WANT TO ATTRACT STUDENTS BY "SELLING" THE IMAGE OF CERTAIN COLLEGES TO MAKE THEIR "BRANDS" ATTRACTIVE.

KAMENETZ ALSO SAYS THAT SUPPLY AND DEMAND IS ONLY PART OF THE STORY.

THAT DEMAND IS ALSO DRIVEN UP BY LOAN POLICIES THAT MAKE A LARGE AMOUNT OF CREDIT AVAILABLE TO YOUNG BORROWERS AS LONG AS THEY USE IT FOR COLLEGE.

IN ADDITION TO ECONOMIC FACTORS, LOTS OF OTHER FACTORS ARE IN-VOLVED IN HOW COLLEGES ARE PRICED.

PLUS, THERE ARE POLITICAL AND EMOTIONAL FACTORS THAT CAN BE HARD TO BOIL DOWN TO NUMBERS.

LEGACY
STATUS
EMOTIONS
DUTY
PRESTIGE

OKAY, BUT I'M NOT SURE I GOT THAT PART ABOUT COMPARING THE COST OF HIGHER EDUCATION TO THE COST OF HEALTH CARE...

WELL, LET'S TAKE A LOOK AT THAT PASSAGE.

SHE'S USING EVIDENCE TO SUPPORT HER CLAIM. SHE QUOTES AN ECONOMIST NAMED RICK MATTOON -- TWICE!

BUT WHAT DOES **HEALTH CARE** HAVE TO DO WITH ANYTHING?

THE BIG CLAIM SHE IS PRESENTING IS HERE IN HER TOPIC SENTENCE: SUPPLY AND DEMAND CAN BE MANIPULATED BY COLLEGES.

WE HAVE TO RELY ON THE COLLEGES TO PROVIDE US WITH INFORMATION ABOUT HOW THEY WILL SPEND OUR MONEY.

WE DON'T KNOW WHY OUR COLLEGE CHARGES WHAT IT CHARGES OR WHETHER HIGHER TUITION MEANS THAT WE'LL GET A BETTER EDUCATION.

Supply and demand, for one thing, can be manipulated. "There's a system bias: this is imperfect information economics," says Rick Mattoon, an economist at the Federal Reserve Bank of Chicago and an expert on the economics of higher education. Markets function best when both buyers and sellers are well informed. When either side is missing information, prices are likely to be too low or too high. In health care, for example, comparison shopping is difficult because patients lack expertise about the relative benefits of various treatments. In the case of education too, Mattoon argues, "There's very little transparency. The schools have all the power. As an applicant you have to tell them everything about your financial situation, your ability to pay for the education, and they tell you nothing about their cost of supplying it. It's even worse than an airline," where people sitting in adjoining seats may have paid very different fares. "In higher ed everyone is paying a radically different price for the same good. . . . If you want to get suspicious about it, it's cartel behavior."

College administrators don't like being referred to as a cartel, a group that colludes to set prices. Their preferred excuse for raising tuition is their own operating costs, especially wages. . . .

I GET IT. IT'S AN **ANALOGY.** ONE DOCTOR MIGHT ORDER EXPENSIVE TESTS WHILE ANOTHER ONE MIGHT SEND YOU HOME WITH TWO ASPIRIN.

YOU HAVE TO TRUST THAT THE DOCTOR YOU PICK WILL RECOMMEND THE BEST THING FOR YOU.

AND LOOK AT THE **RHETORICAL STRATEGY** THAT KAMENETZ IS USING HERE, MAKING LIVELY COMPARISONS TO THE HEALTH CARE SYSTEM AND THEN TO THE AIRLINE INDUSTRY.

COMING UP IN THE NEXT EXCITING EPISODE OF **REFRAME** → "Get a CLUE!" [pg. 207]

DRAWING CONCLUSIONS

The following assignments ask you to
think about creating effective arguments.

 Map out the financial and personal costs of your
college education and the financial and personal
gains you hope to get from it. Use both text
and visuals to present compelling information
about your college costs.

What argument do you think your map
is making? Write a few paragraphs
explaining how you would persuade an
interested audience (such as a family
member) that your studies are -- or
are not -- worthwhile.

 Think about the various ways in which students highlight and otherwise
graphically engage with their books. Pick a paragraph from an academic
or personal argument you have written recently. Mark up the material,
using highlighters of different colors, sticky notes, annotations, or other
methods, to identify topic sentences, supporting claims,
and data, along with any counterarguments.

What does such annotation tell you about how
you developed your argument? What might
you do differently to revise the work and, if
necessary, create a more balanced argument?

3 Proving causality often requires consideration of multiple factors and complex processes. Focus on some aspect of a contemporary issue (such as cyberbullying) that interests you and brainstorm with a partner about the various possible causes and effects. Can you suggest other potential causes of a given effect? What evidence might support the idea that an effect actually springs from a cause you identify?

Write or sketch out a chain of causes and effects leading to and from the issue on which you are focusing, and make notes on at least two points that will help you better understand or address the issue. What information would you need to convince classmates that your explanation of causes and effects makes sense? For instance, you might trace the various causes that have led people to believe that cyberbullying is a serious Internet issue -- while you also investigate the perspective of those who think the issue isn't a particularly serious problem.

4 Create a plan for a Web site that would discuss in an engaging way the issue you identified in assignment 3. How would you show the seriousness (or lack of seriousness) of the issue to a particular audience? What evidence would you need to include on the site, and how would you present that evidence -- using links? text? images? media files? How would you organize the site?

Present your plan to a small group of classmates and collect feedback on your site proposal.

bedfordstmartins.com/understandingrhetoric

Issue 5 • Research: More Than Detective Work

Successful DETECTION & RESEARCH tips!

START

Distinguish between PRIMARY and SECONDARY sources

RESEARCH as widely as possible

READ as much of each SOURCE as possible

EVALUATE your sources

★ LOSE A TURN! ★

SUMMARIZE or PARAPHRASE your sources-- in your OWN WORDS!

Select useful QUOTATIONS

★ ROLL AGAIN! ★

Exercise CAUTION when CUTTING and PASTING SOURCES

GO BACK TO START

A+

Always CITE SOURCES

★ GO BACK 2 SPACES ★

BUT IF YOU WRITE A TELL-ALL BOOK YEARS LATER, THAT WON'T BE A PRIMARY SOURCE ANY MORE.

RIGHT?

ACTUALLY, IF I WITNESSED OR PARTICIPATED IN AN EVENT, HISTORIANS WOULD CONSIDER MY ACCOUNT A **PRIMARY SOURCE**...

...NO MATTER WHEN THE ACCOUNT WAS WRITTEN.

EXPERIMENTAL RESULTS AND FIELD RESEARCH ARE ALSO PRIMARY SOURCES THAT OTHER RESEARCHERS CAN BUILD ON.

GOVERNMENT DOCUMENTS CAN BE IMPORTANT PRIMARY SOURCES FOR RESEARCH PROJECTS AS WELL.

A PRIMARY SOURCE DOESN'T NEED TO BE A WRITTEN TEXT, EITHER.

PAINTINGS, SOUND RECORDINGS, FILMS, BUILDINGS -- ALL OF THESE AND MORE CAN BE PRIMARY SOURCES YOU MIGHT EXPLORE IN A CLASS OR IN OTHER WRITING CONTEXTS.

BLUEPRINTS

A **SECONDARY SOURCE** IS A SOURCE THAT DESCRIBES, ANALYZES, OR INTERPRETS A PRIMARY SOURCE.

BOOKS AND ARTICLES ABOUT LITERATURE, SCIENCE, OR ART MIGHT BE CONSIDERED SECONDARY SOURCES.

2

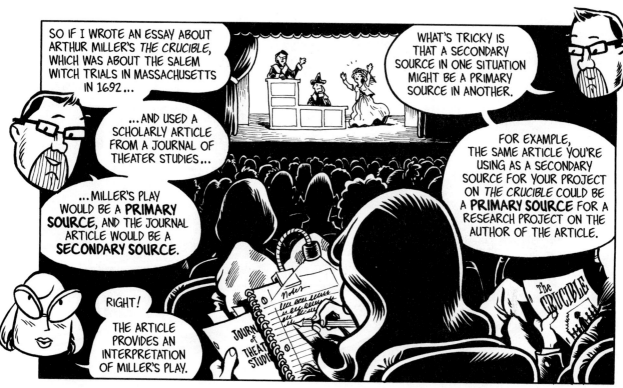

SO IF I WROTE AN ESSAY ABOUT ARTHUR MILLER'S *THE CRUCIBLE*, WHICH WAS ABOUT THE SALEM WITCH TRIALS IN MASSACHUSETTS IN 1692...

...AND USED A SCHOLARLY ARTICLE FROM A JOURNAL OF THEATER STUDIES...

...MILLER'S PLAY WOULD BE A **PRIMARY SOURCE**, AND THE JOURNAL ARTICLE WOULD BE A **SECONDARY SOURCE**.

RIGHT! THE ARTICLE PROVIDES AN INTERPRETATION OF MILLER'S PLAY.

WHAT'S TRICKY IS THAT A SECONDARY SOURCE IN ONE SITUATION MIGHT BE A PRIMARY SOURCE IN ANOTHER.

FOR EXAMPLE, THE SAME ARTICLE YOU'RE USING AS A SECONDARY SOURCE FOR YOUR PROJECT ON *THE CRUCIBLE* COULD BE A **PRIMARY SOURCE** FOR A RESEARCH PROJECT ON THE AUTHOR OF THE ARTICLE.

A SUBJECT LIKE THE SALEM WITCH TRIALS CAN INTEREST RESEARCHERS IN MANY FIELDS.

INDEED, SCHOLARS LOOK FOR DIFFERENT KINDS OF EVIDENCE IN APPROACHING THE SAME SUBJECT...

...AND THEY MAY EVEN DRAW DIFFERENT CONCLUSIONS FROM THE SAME EVIDENCE.

HISTORIANS WHO STUDY RACE LOOK AT HOW PERCEIVED RACIAL DIFFERENCES AND STEREOTYPES ABOUT SLAVES MIGHT HAVE PLAYED INTO THE PURITANS' HYSTERIA ABOUT WITCHES.

HOWEVER, SCHOLARS DISAGREE ABOUT THE ETHNICITIES OF THE TOWN'S RESIDENTS AND HOW RACE WAS PERCEIVED IN 1690s NEW ENGLAND.

ETHNO-HISTORY

ECONOMISTS MIGHT LOOK AT SUPPLY AND DEMAND TO UNDERSTAND THE EVENTS THAT TOOK PLACE IN SALEM VILLAGE, PARTICULARLY WHEN CROPS FAILED OR VILLAGERS SQUABBLED OVER PROPERTY RIGHTS.

SOMETIMES EVEN THE "FACTS" OF HISTORICAL CASES MAY BE OPEN TO DEBATE.

RAINFALL STATISTICS AND THE LOCATIONS OF PROPERTY LINES WEREN'T RECORDED AS CAREFULLY IN 1692 AS THEY ARE TODAY.

JOURNAL of ECONOMIC PERSPECTIVE

SOME SCHOLARS HAVE ARGUED THAT THE AFFLICTED PEOPLE OF SALEM WERE ACTUALLY HALLUCINATING AFTER EATING CONTAMINATED RYE.

RYE BREAD

YOU SHOULD CONSULT MULTIPLE SOURCES TO GET A SENSE OF THE SCHOLARLY DEBATES SURROUNDING YOUR RESEARCH TOPIC. NOT EVERYONE AGREES THAT WHAT THE PURITANS ATE WAS TO BLAME FOR THE SALEM WITCH HYSTERIA.

JOURNAL of RYE
R.Q. RYE QUARTERLY
STUDY: Rye Best for Grilled Cheese

CAST A WIDE NET FOR YOUR RESEARCH AND READ THROUGH ALL THE LIBRARY RECORDS OR SEARCH SCREENS. DON'T STOP AT THE FIRST PAGE OF RESULTS.

OF COURSE, IF YOU TURN UP THOUSANDS OF GOOGLE HITS, YOU NEED TO NARROW YOUR SEARCH, BEFORE YOU READ THROUGH THE RESULTS.

HMMM...

BIBLIOGRAPHY
Aaronson, Albert
Alabaster, Arthur
Amand, Alexandra
Anderson, Alice
April, Anders
Arlington, Alan
Atwood, Ambrose
that's it!

DECIDING WHICH SOURCES TO TRUST

Jonathan Alexander says:
HOWEVER, THERE ARE SOME SITUATIONS WHERE ONLINE SOURCES WITH A STRONG SELF-INTEREST, SUCH AS TWEETS AND STATUS UPDATES, MAY GIVE AN INSIDER'S VIEW OF CURRENT EVENTS.

@Lizlosh
THINK ABOUT WHICH SOURCES WILL BEST SERVE YOUR PURPOSE IN THIS CONTEXT.

89/160 Remaining

YOU CAN ALSO LOOK FOR INFORMATION ABOUT THE CREATOR OF A POTENTIAL SOURCE.

IS THIS PERSON A SCHOLAR, AN EXPERT, OR AN INFORMED OBSERVER? HOW CAN YOU FIND OUT?

IF THE PERSON TEACHES AT A UNIVERSITY, YOU MIGHT LOOK AT HIS OR HER FACULTY WEB PAGE.

Alexander, Jonathan

Professor of English and Director of the Center for Excellence in Writing and Communication at the University of California, Irvine.

IT MIGHT GIVE YOU A BETTER SENSE OF THE SCHOLAR'S PERSONALITY, RESEARCH INTERESTS, AND DEPTH OF KNOWLEDGE ON THE SUBJECT.

A WRITER REGARDED AS AN EXPERT MAY OFTEN BE CITED BY OTHERS.

To: Luis
From: Cindy

Hey, check o[...]
this blog abou[...]
Arthur Mille[...]
It's RAD!
http://www.arthur[...]
Later!
Cindy

REPLY   DELETE

Reference + Information

A LIBRARY'S CATALOG AND DATABASES CAN SHOW THE ACADEMIC WORK THAT A PARTICULAR AUTHOR HAS PUBLISHED.

YOU CAN USE AN INTER-NET SEARCH ENGINE TO FIND OUT ABOUT WRITERS WHO AREN'T ACADEMICS.

MANY AUTHORS HAVE PERSONAL WEB PAGES WITH INFORMATION ABOUT THEIR WORK.

CHECK A SOURCE'S DATE OF PUBLICATION.

A RECENT BOOK OR ARTICLE IS LIKELY TO CONTAIN REFERENCES TO THE MOST CURRENT RESEARCH.

DISCIPLINES SUCH AS THE SCIENCES MAY REQUIRE UP-TO-DATE SOURCES, SINCE KNOWLEDGE IN THOSE DISCIPLINES CHANGES RAPIDLY.

the BENEFITS of LEECHES 1756

IN OTHER DISCIPLINES, SUCH AS HISTORY, OLDER ACCOUNTS MIGHT SOMETIMES BE APPROPRIATE.

A WORD OF CAUTION: THINK CARE-FULLY ABOUT POPULAR PERIODICALS.

IF YOUR BEST SOURCE IS A NEWS-PAPER ARTICLE, YOU SHOULD PROBABLY KEEP LOOKING.

POPULAR NEWS
She Sings!

JOURNALISTS OFTEN HAVE GOOD GENERAL KNOWLEDGE...

...AND GOOD WRITING SKILLS...

BUT MOST REPORTERS AREN'T SPECIALISTS WITH IN-DEPTH KNOWLEDGE OF THE TOPIC.

INSTEAD, SEE IF THE NEWSPAPER ARTICLE MENTIONS A PROFESSOR, A GOVERNMENT OFFICIAL, OR ANOTHER EXPERT ON THE TOPIC, AND THEN SEARCH FOR INFORMATION FROM THESE SPECIFIC SOURCES.

ADS

SUMMARY   PARAPHRASE   QUOTATION

SETTING UP CONTEXTS AND PROVIDING BACKGROUND INFORMATION

GIVING A SENSE OF THE AUTHOR'S ARGUMENT

DRAWING ATTENTION TO SOMETHING PARTICULARLY EVOCATIVE OR INSIGHTFUL IN THE AUTHOR'S OWN WORDS

LET'S TALK ABOUT SUMMARIZING, PARAPHRASING, AND QUOTING -- HOW TO DO THEM, WHEN, AND WHY.

SUMMARIZING

PRESENTS A CONCISE, GENERAL SENSE OF WHAT YOUR SOURCE IS ABOUT.

OFTEN, SUMMARIZING GIVES A BROAD OVERVIEW OF MATERIAL THAT IS NOT IN DISPUTE.

HERE'S A SUMMARY THAT USES CONTENT FROM A WIKIPEDIA ARTICLE:

"The history of detective fiction dates back to 1841, when Edgar Allan Poe introduced Monsieur C. Auguste Dupin in the short story 'The Murders in the Rue Morgue.' Today it includes the police procedural, the legal thriller, the courtroom drama, the locked room mystery, hard-boiled fiction, the noir novel, and the 'cozy,' in which sex and violence are downplayed. In the 'cozy,' the protagonist is often a female amateur, and humor and social satire might be important parts of the narrative."

REMEMBER #1 **SUMMARIZE** to set up CONTEXTS and provide background INFORMATION.

PARAPHRASING SHOULD GIVE THE READER A MORE COMPLETE SENSE OF THE AUTHOR'S ARGUMENT AND MORE OF THE FLAVOR OF THE ORIGINAL THAN A SUMMARY.

AND EVEN THOUGH A PARAPHRASE IS "IN YOUR OWN WORDS," THE IDEAS CAME FROM SOMEWHERE ELSE -- SO YOU'LL HAVE TO CITE YOUR SOURCE.

HERE'S A PARAPHRASE OF PART OF A CHAPTER IN THE BOOK CITY OF QUARTZ, A HISTORY OF LOS ANGELES.

AUTHOR MIKE DAVIS CLAIMS THAT NOIR STORIES ABOUT CRIME AND THE ILL EFFECTS OF CAPITALISM REFLECT MANY DIFFERENT INFLU- ENCES FROM THE TIME OF THE GREAT DEPRESSION, WORLD WAR II, AND THE PERIOD THAT FOLLOWED.

DAVIS ARGUES THAT IMMIGRANT WRITERS, COMPOSERS, FILMMAKERS, AND ARTISTS FLEEING HITLER'S GERMANY PLAYED A ROLE IN DEVELOPING CERTAIN ASPECTS OF THE NOIR DETECTIVE GENRE, BUT HE INSISTS THAT FEW OF THEM ACTUALLY PARTICIPATED IN THE GRITTY URBAN LIFESTYLES OF LOS ANGELES IN THE 1940s.

UNLIKE MANY CRITICS, DAVIS ASSERTS THAT LOCAL LOS ANGELES AUTHORS PLAYED A MAJOR ROLE IN DEVELOP- ING WHAT CAME TO BE KNOWN AS "L.A. NOIR."

HE SAYS THAT THESE LOCAL WRITERS KNEW MUCH MORE ABOUT THE SCANDALS OF THE CITY -- POLICE CORRUPTION, REAL ESTATE AND OIL SPECULATION, AND ANTI-LABOR AND ANTI-IMMIGRANT POLITICS -- THAN OUTSIDERS COMING FROM EUROPE DID.

WOW!

THAT PARAPHRASE REALLY GAVE ME A SENSE OF DAVIS'S ARGUMENT AND OF WHY HIS SCHOLARSHIP IS DISTINCTIVE.

SO, WHEN YOU FIND A SOURCE THAT IS REALLY SIGNIFICANT FOR YOUR RESEARCH, EVEN IF YOU DISAGREE WITH IT, YOU MIGHT WANT TO SPEND SOME TIME CAREFULLY PARAPHRASING IT IN YOUR OWN WORDS.

PARAPHRASE

SUMMARY

REMEMBER #2

PARAPHRASE
to give a sense of the author's ARGUMENT.

NOW, **QUOTING** COMES IN HANDY WHEN YOUR SOURCES SAY SOMETHING PARTICULARLY EVOCATIVE...

...OR **INSIGHTFUL**...

...OR WHEN YOU WANT TO CALL ATTENTION TO A WRITER'S **LANGUAGE**.

GENIUS!

YOU CAN QUOTE A SHORT PASSAGE OR EVEN JUST A SIGNIFICANT KEYWORD.

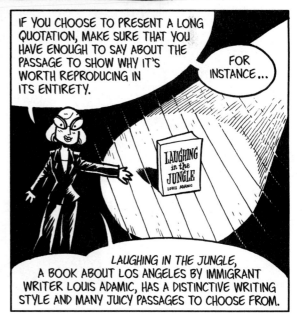

IF YOU CHOOSE TO PRESENT A LONG QUOTATION, MAKE SURE THAT YOU HAVE ENOUGH TO SAY ABOUT THE PASSAGE TO SHOW WHY IT'S WORTH REPRODUCING IN ITS ENTIRETY.

FOR INSTANCE...

LAUGHING in the JUNGLE
LOUIS ADAMIC

LAUGHING IN THE JUNGLE, A BOOK ABOUT LOS ANGELES BY IMMIGRANT WRITER LOUIS ADAMIC, HAS A DISTINCTIVE WRITING STYLE AND MANY JUICY PASSAGES TO CHOOSE FROM.

HERE ARE ADAMIC'S PROVOCATIVE INSIGHTS ON THE CITY:

"FROM MOUNT HOLLYWOOD, LOS ANGELES LOOKS RATHER NICE....

"ACTUALLY, AND IN SPITE OF ALL THE HEALTHFUL SUNSHINE AND OCEAN BREEZES, IT IS A **BAD** PLACE, FULL OF OLD, DYING PEOPLE, AND YOUNG PEOPLE WHO WERE BORN OLD OF TIRED PIONEER PARENTS, VICTIMS OF AMERICA --

"-- FULL OF CURIOUS WILD AND POISONOUS GROWTHS, DECADENT RELIGIONS AND CULTS AND FAKE SCIENCE, AND WILDCAT BUSINESS ENTERPRISES, WHICH, WITH THEIR AIM FOR QUICK PROFITS, ARE DOOMED TO COLLAPSE AND DRAG DOWN MULTITUDES OF PEOPLE...

"... A JUNGLE."

IF YOU DON'T NEED THE WHOLE QUOTATION, YOU CAN WEAVE SHORT QUOTED DESCRIPTIONS INTO YOUR OWN PROSE.

NOTICE THAT, IN EACH CASE, WE USE QUOTATION MARKS, PROVIDE AN IN-TEXT CITATION (THIS ONE FOLLOWS MLA STYLE), AND EMPHASIZE OUR OWN COMMENTARY.

"Adamic gives us verbal images that contradict a popular picture of health. Terms such as 'poisonous,' 'dying,' and 'decadent' (220) provide a stark contrast with the 'sunshine and ocean breezes' typically associated with L.A."

tap tap

REMEMBER #3

QUOTE
to draw attention to the author's own WORDS and PHRASING.

*In this case, Tom Gammill, creator of The Doozies.

YOU SHOULD **TALK** TO US IF YOU'RE HAVING TROUBLE HANDLING A PROJECT.

PRESENTING OTHERS' WORK AS YOUR OWN IS A TERRIBLE IDEA FOR A LOT OF REASONS.

FOR ONE THING, IT'S **PLAGIARISM**.

BUT JUST A COUPLE OF PAGES BACK YOU GUYS WERE TALKING ABOUT QUOTING FROM SOURCES.

BUT YOU NEED TO TELL READERS WHERE YOU FOUND YOUR SOURCES, NOT PRETEND YOU CREATED THE WORK YOURSELF.

AND YOU ALSO NEED TO EVALUATE AND INTERPRET MATERIAL THAT YOU FIND AND INTEGRATE IT INTO YOUR OWN TEXT.

YOU DON'T JUST INSERT SOURCES WITHOUT ANY ANALYSIS OR REFLECTION!

IF YOU ARE GOING TO QUOTE SOMEONE ELSE'S WORK, HAVE A GOOD REASON FOR REPRODUCING IT EXACTLY.

≡SIGH≡

THAT MAKES SENSE.

I GUESS WE KNEW ALL THAT, BUT DESPERATION MAKES PEOPLE DO CRAZY THINGS SOMETIMES.

IT'S NOT ALWAYS EASY TO CITE YOUR SOURCES.

OUR STUDENTS HAVE TROUBLE WITH IT ALL THE TIME.

HOW DO I CITE A VIDEO I WATCHED **ONLINE**?

WHAT ABOUT A **COMIC**?

REFRAME with Luis & Cindy

Get a CLUE!

I HOPE COMING TO THE LIBRARY WASN'T A WASTE OF TIME.

SEARCHING ON GOOGLE MIGHT WORK JUST AS WELL.

DEPENDS ON THE SUBJECT, I GUESS.

Search

Gay Gene

SEARCH CLICK

HMM...

THERE'S ALWAYS **WIKIPEDIA**... BUT SOME OF MY INSTRUCTORS DON'T WANT ME TO USE IT AS A SOURCE.

WHAT ABOUT THIS? "THE 'GAY GENE' EXPLAINED"...

Pictures

Videos

Breaking News

Commerce

Maps

The "Gay Gene" Explained   CLICK

The Gay Gene: A Sociological Review

Welcome to Savior Science!

GIVE THE "ADVANCED SEARCH" OPTIONS A SHOT.

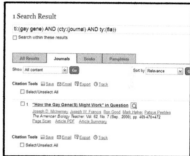

OH, NO.

THIS LOOKS PRETTY COMPLICATED.

TRY "GAY GENE" AS AN ITEM TITLE SO THAT THE PHRASE "GAY GENE" HAS TO BE PART OF THE TITLE.

ADVANCED SEARCH CAN ALSO LIMIT THE RESULTS TO ARTICLES.

I ONLY GOT ONE HIT FROM THAT SEARCH.

BUT IT'S IN A JOURNAL PUBLISHED BY THE NATIONAL ASSOCIATION OF BIOLOGY TEACHERS.

SOUNDS CREDIBLE.

BUT LOOK AT IT TO BE SURE.

OKAY.

CLICK!

1. **Genetic Models of Homosexuality: Generating Testable Predictions** 🔍
Sergey Gavrilets, William R. Rice
Proceedings: Biological Sciences, Vol. 273, No. 1605 (Dec. 22, 2006), pp. 3031-3038
Page Scan   Article PDF   Article Summary

2. **Aquinas on Natural Law and the Virtues in Biblical Context: Homosexuality as a Test Case** 🔍
Eugene F. Rogers Jr.
The Journal of Religious Ethics, Vol. 27, No. 1 (Spring, 1999), pp. 29-56
Page Scan   Article PDF   Article Summary

3. **Beliefs about the Origins of Homosexuality and Support for Gay Rights: An Empirical Test of Attribution Theory**
Donald P. Haider-Markel, Mark R. Joslyn
The Public Opinion Quarterly, Vol. 72, No. 2 (Summer, 2008), pp. 291-310

4. **Scientifi... ...alyses of Homosexuality: A... ...Method...**
Stephen J...
The Journal of Rel... ...Ethics, Vol. 25, No. 1 (Spring, 1997), pp. 89...
Page Scan   Article PDF   Article Summary

THIS TEAM WROTE TWO ARTICLES IN THIS LIST. WHO ARE THEY?

5. **Attributions and the Regulation of Marriage: Considering the Parallels between Race and Homosexuality** 🔍
Donald P. Haider-Markel, Mark R. Joslyn
PS: Political Science and Politics, Vol. 38, No. 2 (Apr., 2005), pp. 233-239
Page Scan   Article PDF   Article Summary

6. **Male Homosexuality: Absence of Linkage to Microsatellite Markers at Xq28** 🔍
George Rice, Carol Anderson, Neil Risch, George Ebers
Science, New Series, Vol. 284, No. 5414 (Apr. 23, 1999), pp. 665-66...
Page Scan   Article PDF   Article Summary

TOO TECHNICAL.

211

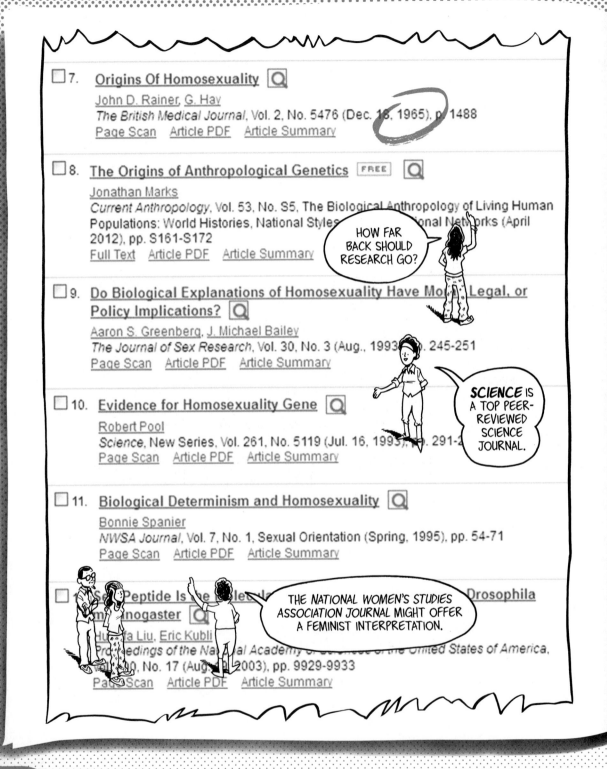

7. **Origins Of Homosexuality**

John D. Rainer, G. Hav
The British Medical Journal, Vol. 2, No. 5476 (Dec. 18, 1965), p. 1488
Page Scan   Article PDF   Article Summary

8. **The Origins of Anthropological Genetics** FREE

Jonathan Marks
Current Anthropology, Vol. 53, No. S5, The Biological Anthropology of Living Human Populations: World Histories, National Styles, ... ional Networks (April 2012), pp. S161-S172
Full Text   Article PDF   Article Summary

9. **Do Biological Explanations of Homosexuality Have Mo... Legal, or Policy Implications?**

Aaron S. Greenberg, J. Michael Bailey
The Journal of Sex Research, Vol. 30, No. 3 (Aug., 1993 245-251
Page Scan   Article PDF   Article Summary

10. **Evidence for Homosexuality Gene**

Robert Pool
Science, New Series, Vol. 261, No. 5119 (Jul. 16, 1993 ... p. 291-2...
Page Scan   Article PDF   Article Summary

11. **Biological Determinism and Homosexuality**

Bonnie Spanier
NWSA Journal, Vol. 7, No. 1, Sexual Orientation (Spring, 1995), pp. 54-71
Page Scan   Article PDF   Article Summary

... **Sex Peptide Is the Molecul... ...** *Drosophila ...anogaster*

Hu...fa Liu, Eric Kubli
Pro...edings of the Na...al Academy ... ...ed States of America, ...0, No. 17 (Aug. ... 2003), pp. 9929-9933
Page Scan   Article PDF   Article Summary

Biological Determinism and Homosexuality

BONNIE SPANIER

State University of New York at Albany

"Why Are Men and Women Different? It isn't just upbringing. New studies show they are born that way." (Gorman)

"Is Homosexuality Born or Bred? Two new studies seem to find the origins of homosexuality in genetics, not parenting." (Gelman)

The recent upsurge in scientific claims about biological bases for male-female differences (including assumed characteristics such as "female intuition") and for differences in sexual orientation (cast as either homosexual or heterosexual) comes from some unexpected quarters. Openly gay or pro-gay scientists have joined traditionally conservative biological determinists and are apparently impelled by reasons ranging from simply feeling they were born gay to recognizing the strength of arguments that if gayness is inborn rather than a lifestyle choice, people cannot be blamed for something over which they have no control. . . . gay rights,

Despite its emergence from worthwhile motives prom . . . says two key [scientific] reception of such biological theories that support racism, . . . of biological . . . erosexism—whe . . . ifference is . . .

YOU CAN CLICK ON THE LINK TO READ THE FULL ARTICLE.

MY CLASS IS STUDYING GENDER QUESTIONS, SO THIS MIGHT BE JUST WHAT I NEED.

Works Cited

A . . . Laura S., M. Hines, J. E. Shryne, and R. A. Gorski. "Two Sexually . . . orphic Cell Groups in the Human Brain." *Journal of Neuroscience* 9 (1989): . . . –506.

. . . er, Natalie . . . n Fish, Social Status . . . " *New York Times* . . . Nov. 1991: . . . C12.

→ Barinaga, Marcia. " . . .

Bleier, Ruth. "A De . . . (Autumn 1988) . . .

———. *Science an* . . .
Bleier, Ruth, L . . .
Gender, Age . . .
8 (1986): 391 . . .
Burr, Chandler. . . .
65.

AND IF AN ARTICLE SEEMS CREDIBLE AND USEFUL FOR YOUR RESEARCH, LOOK AT THE SOURCES IT CITES TO FIND MORE EXAMPLES OF WHAT YOU'RE LOOKING FOR.

HEY, THAT'S A PRETTY GOOD TRICK FOR FINDING MORE SOURCES.

WHO KNEW THAT THE LIBRARY HELD SO MANY SECRETS?

COMING UP IN THE NEXT EXCITING EPISODE OF **REFRAME**

"Am I MISSING something?"

[pg. 237]

DRAWING CONCLUSIONS

The following assignments ask you to practice finding,
evaluating, and responding to research sources.

1 Choose a historical event that interests you. Conduct an Internet search to get an overview of the kinds of sources on that subject that you can find outside the library. (Keep track of the search terms you use, and make a note of those that seem to produce the most effective results.)

Bookmark the information that seems most current, most reliable, and most intriguing. What makes you trust or distrust the sources you find?

2 Create a research log to follow up on the event you investigated in assignment 1. Collect and organize the citation information about each Internet source that you consider or even look at briefly. Now go to the library and discuss the information you've gathered so far with a research librarian.

What other kinds of sources does the library offer -- database articles, special collections -- that you can't find online? Find at least five library sources that may be useful for your project and record bibliographic information and a brief summary of each. (If you like, you can use a camera or phone to record visual and audio notes about books, images, and people relevant to your project.)

3

Find at least two primary sources with first-person accounts of the historical event you began investigating in assignment 1. (Remember that illustrations and other images can be primary sources, too.)

Lay out a storyboard that illustrates those accounts of the event and shows how they relate to each other. Do they depict the event from similar perspectives? Do they differ in significant ways? Create a brief explanation of the questions that you uncover in examining these different accounts.

4

A good way to begin creating a research-based argument is to find a position that you will refute or critique. Think about your position on some significant aspect of the event you have begun researching. (In this chapter, for instance, Jonathan and Liz explore different explanations for the witchcraft hysteria around Salem Village.)

Find a source -- perhaps one that is already part of the research log you began in assignment 2 -- that takes a thoughtful position that differs from your own. Summarize that source's argument fairly, and then sketch out a chart or an outline of your response.

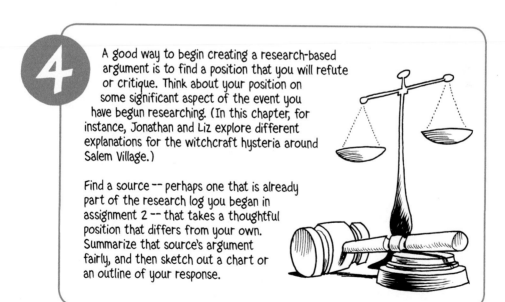

bedfordstmartins.com/understandingrhetoric

ISSUE 6
RETHINKING REVISION
In this issue...
LOOKING BEYOND THE RED INK
Page 218
REVIEWING RHETORICALLY
Page 223
SEEING THROUGH OTHERS' EYES
Page 226
REVISING RADICALLY
Page 230
ital
stet
-30-

LOOKING FOR ERRORS THAT ARE DISTRACTING, EVEN IF THEY DON'T SERIOUSLY INTERFERE WITH READERS' UNDERSTANDING, IS ONLY THE MOST BASIC FORM OF REVISION.

BUT EVEN IF FLAWS AREN'T SERIOUS, THEY CAN MAKE YOU LOOK **TERRIBLE**.

YOU CAN'T JUST IGNORE WHAT EVERYONE CAN SEE PLAINLY.

PEOPLE MIGHT NOT SAY ANY-THING TO YOUR FACE, BUT THEY WILL CERTAINLY JUDGE YOU IF YOU LOOK BAD.

SO-CALLED "SURFACE ERRORS" CAN BE A TURN-OFF TO AUDIENCES.

LIKE ITS AND IT'S. WHY CAN'T PEOPLE GET THAT RIGHT?

OR THEIR, THEY'RE, AND THERE.

I HATE THAT MISTAKE.

LOOK, WE UNDERSTAND.

WE'RE WRITING TEACHERS. WE SEE MISTAKES ALL DAY LONG.

SOME COMMON ERRORS ARE ALSO VERY DISTRACTING.

OUR FRIEND ELLEN STRENSKI CALLS THESE "NOSE-PICKING ERRORS."

SUCH ERRORS SEEM TO INDICATE A LACK OF SELF-AWARENESS.

AND THEY SIGNAL THAT THE PEOPLE WHO MAKE THEM EITHER DON'T KNOW CONVENTIONS OF ACADEMIC WRITING OR WON'T SHOW THEIR AUDIENCES ENOUGH RESPECT TO EDIT THE WORK CAREFULLY.

SOME PEOPLE FIND THESE ERRORS SO REPULSIVE THAT THEY CAN'T PAY ATTENTION TO THE MESSAGE BEING DELIVERED.

THESE PEOPLE MAY BE OVERLY SENSITIVE ABOUT IMPERFECTION...

...BUT YOU WANT TO AVOID UNINTENTIONALLY CREATING STRONG NEGATIVE REACTIONS TO YOUR WRITING.

221

PRETTY MUCH ALL OF THE BOOKS IN THIS LIBRARY WERE REVISED DURING THE DRAFTING PROCESS IN WAYS THAT WENT FAR BEYOND SIMPLY FIXING SPELLING AND GRAMMATICAL MISTAKES.

SEE THIS BOOK?

IT'S PERSUASION, JANE AUSTEN'S LAST NOVEL. THE INITIAL DRAFT OF THIS BOOK HAD A COMPLETELY DIFFERENT ENDING.

Persuasion
JANE AUSTEN
1775-1817

THE ORIGINAL ENDING DIDN'T HAVE THE WITTY DIALOGUE OR THE OBSERVATIONS ABOUT HUMAN CHARACTER THAT AUSTEN WAS KNOWN FOR.

THE FIRST VERSION OF AUSTEN'S HAPPY ENDING COMES ABOUT BECAUSE THE HEROINE IS TRICKED INTO BEING ALONE WITH THE HERO. WHEN HE DECLARES HIS LOVE FOR HER IN VERY CONVENTIONAL LANGUAGE, SHE DOESN'T HAVE MUCH TO SAY IN RESPONSE.

BECAUSE AUSTEN WASN'T HAPPY WITH THE ENDING OF HER NOVEL, SHE REVISED RADICALLY.

SHE CREATED A BRAND-NEW SCENE IN WHICH A LOT WAS GOING ON BECAUSE THE CHARACTERS IN THE STORY WERE PREPARING FOR A WEDDING.

Mary and Henrietta heading out the front door for a walk.

Mrs. Musgrove giving Mrs. Croft the history of her eldest daughter's engagement.

Captain Wentworth secretly writing a love letter to Anne.

Captain Harville and Anne arguing about whether men or women are more faithful.

IN THE REVISED ENDING, AUSTEN'S HEROINE SHOWS HERSELF TO BE A SOPHISTICATED CONVERSATIONALIST IN A DEBATE ABOUT WHETHER MEN OR WOMEN ARE MORE FAITHFUL IN LOVE.

ALTHOUGH HE DOESN'T SEEM TO BE PAYING ATTENTION, THE DASHING HERO IS ACTUALLY LISTENING TO HER ARGUMENT ATTENTIVELY.

WHILE ALL THE ACTION IS GOING ON AROUND HIM, HE WRITES HER A LETTER TO TELL HER HOW HE REALLY FEELS.

I DEFINITELY LIKE THAT ENDING BETTER.

IT IS A LOT MORE RHETORICALLY INTERESTING.

OF COURSE, A MORE ELABORATE SOLUTION TO A PROBLEM IN A PIECE OF WRITING ISN'T ALWAYS THE RIGHT APPROACH.

SOMETIMES A SIMPLER SOLUTION IS BETTER.

TEMPUS FUGIT

BUT WHETHER YOU'RE REVISING A NOVEL OR A PIECE OF ACADEMIC WRITING...

...IT'S IMPORTANT TO GIVE YOURSELF ENOUGH TIME TO MAKE MAJOR REVISIONS, AS AUSTEN DID.

SEEING THROUGH OTHERS' EYES

OFTEN WRITERS CONSULT OTHER WRITERS FOR HELP WHEN MAKING A MAJOR REVISION.

IN A WRITING CLASS, THIS PROCESS MIGHT BE CALLED "PEER EDITING" OR "PEER REVISION."

U.S. PRESIDENT ABRAHAM LINCOLN'S SECRETARY OF STATE, WILLIAM SEWARD, WAS VERY IMPORTANT IN THE REVISION OF LINCOLN'S MAJOR SPEECHES.

SEWARD THOUGHT THAT IT WAS IMPORTANT FOR LINCOLN'S FIRST INAUGURAL SPEECH TO AVOID A CONFRONTATIONAL TONE THAT WOULD ANGER THE LOSING CANDIDATE'S SUPPORTERS.

SPEECHES OF ABRAHAM LINCOLN

HE WORRIED THAT LINCOLN MIGHT SAY SOMETHING THAT COULD BE INTERPRETED AS AN EXCUSE FOR THE SOUTH TO SECEDE FROM THE UNION.

ABRAHAM LINCOLN (1809–1865)
16th PRESIDENT OF THE UNITED STATES

WILLIAM HENRY SEWARD (1801–1872)
SECRETARY OF STATE

SEWARD WAS RIGHT TO BE WORRIED. LINCOLN'S EARLY DRAFTS FOR THE INAUGURAL ADDRESS WERE EXTREMELY CONFRONTATIONAL.

In your hands, my dissatisfied fellow countrymen, and not in mine, is the momentous issue of civil war. The government will not assail you, unless you first assail it. You can have no conflict, without being yourselves the aggressors. You have no oath registered in Heaven to destroy the government, while I shall have the most solemn one to "preserve, protect, and defend" it. You can forbear the assault upon it; I can not shrink from the defense of it. With you, and not with me, is the solemn question of "Shall it be peace, or a sword?"

HE'S PRACTICALLY DARING SLAVEHOLDING STATES TO REVOLT.

"SHALL IT BE PEACE, OR A SWORD?" WHAT A TERRIBLE ENDING!

WHAT IS HE **THINKING**?

SEWARD LATER EXPLAINED WHAT HE SAW AS THE FLAW IN LINCOLN'S ORIGINAL APPROACH:

...we must CHANGE THE QUESTION BEFORE THE PUBLIC FROM ONE UPON SLAVERY, OR ABOUT SLAVERY, for a question upon UNION OR DISUNION.

227

SEWARD KNEW THAT THE FINAL WORDS OF THE SPEECH WERE GOING TO HAVE THE MOST RHETORICAL IMPACT. SO HE OFFERED THE PRESIDENT SOME DIFFERENT OPTIONS FOR WORDING AND SUGGESTED TWO DIFFERENT ENDINGS.

LIKE ANY GOOD PEER REVIEWER, SEWARD GAVE HIS PARTNER SOME CHOICES.

LINCOLN LIKED THE SECOND OF SEWARD'S SUGGESTED CLOSING PARAGRAPHS BETTER.

The mystic chords which proceeding from so many battle fields and so many patriot graves pass through all the hearts and all the hearths in this broad continent of ours will yet again harmonize in their ancient music when breathed upon by the guardian angel of the nation.

LINCOLN APPROVED OF SEWARD'S COMPLEX METAPHOR OF A MUSICAL STRING CONNECTING TWO POINTS.

THIS RHETORICAL FIGURE REPRESENTED THE EMOTIONAL BOND CONNECTING THE GRAVES OF REVOLUTIONARY SOLDIERS TO THE PEOPLE OF LINCOLN'S OWN DAY.

We are not enemies, but friends.
We must not be enemies.

Though passion may have strained, it must not break our bonds of affection.

The mystic chords of memory, stretching from every battlefield, and patriot grave, to every living heart and hearthstone, all over this broad land, will yet swell the chorus of the Union, when again touched, as surely they will be, by the better angels of our nature.

WHEN YOUR OWN WORK IS REVIEWED BY OTHER PEOPLE, IT CAN BE IMPORTANT TO EVALUATE THEIR SUGGESTIONS.

ACCEPTING ALL ADVICE FROM OTHERS UNCRITICALLY CAN BE ALMOST AS BAD AS REFUSING TO LISTEN TO FEEDBACK IN THE FIRST PLACE.

BE AN ACTIVE PARTICIPANT IN YOUR REVISION PROCESS AT EVERY STAGE OF DRAFTING.

REVISING RADICALLY

LINCOLN WAS A FAMOUSLY CREATIVE REVISER.

LINCOLN'S DRAFTS

HE OFTEN HAD DRAFTS OF HIS SPEECHES PRINTED, SO HE COULD SEE THE LANGUAGE NOT IN HIS OWN HANDWRITING.

THEN HE WOULD CUT UP THESE PRINTED DRAFTS AND REARRANGE THEM.

HE WOULD ALSO SPLICE IN ADDITIONAL HANDWRITTEN REVISIONS.

A LOT HAS CHANGED SINCE THESE REVISERS DEVELOPED THEIR OWN PERSONAL STRATEGIES FOR IMPROVING WRITTEN TEXTS.

REMEMBER THAT THESE FAMOUS WRITERS WERE REVISING FOR DIFFERENT REASONS.

JANE AUSTEN (1775–1817)

ABRAHAM LINCOLN (1809–1865)

AUSTEN WANTED TO IMPROVE HER NARRATIVE AND SOLVE A STRUCTURAL PROBLEM.

LINCOLN WAS FOCUSING ON PERSUADING A SKEPTICAL AUDIENCE.

REVISE REVISE

WE ENCOURAGE YOU TO THINK ABOUT REVISION RADICALLY.

SOMETIMES WRITERS HAVE TO MAKE RADICAL REVISIONS FOR REASONS NOT OF THEIR OWN CHOOSING.

TONIGHT: 7pm Maxine Hong Kingston

WHEN THE MANUSCRIPT OF WRITER MAXINE HONG KINGSTON'S NOVEL-IN-PROGRESS BURNED IN 1991, ALONG WITH HER HOUSE AND ALL HER POSSESSIONS, SHE HAD TO RECONSTITUTE MATERIAL FROM MEMORY. SHE CHOSE TO INCORPORATE THE STORY OF THE FIRE INTO THE FINAL VERSION OF HER NOVEL, CALLED *THE FIFTH BOOK OF PEACE.*

OF COURSE, THIS EXPERIENCE WAS TRAUMATIC FOR KINGSTON.

BUT IT ALSO SHOWS HOW DESTRUCTION MAY SOMETIMES BE A PART OF THE CREATIVE PROCESS.

YOU MIGHT ASK YOURSELF:

IF I COULD ONLY SAVE ONE PARAGRAPH OF THE WORK I'M WRITING, WHICH ONE WOULD I SAVE?

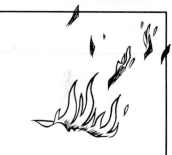

WHICH ONE WOULD I LET GO FIRST?

Cutting and pasting text on a computer screen may seem monotonous, so you might try printing out your work and physically moving the pieces...

YOU MIGHT THINK IT'S TOO LATE TO KEEP INVESTIGATING, BUT RESEARCH* IS AN IMPORTANT PART OF THE REVISION PROCESS.

ARE THERE ANY SOURCES THAT YOU HAVE OVERLOOKED?

ARE THERE ANY SOURCES THAT CAN'T BE TRUSTED?

AND HAVE YOU CREDITED ALL THE DETECTIVE WORK THAT ISN'T YOUR OWN?

*For more on research, see CHAPTER 5.

SOMETIMES IT IS HELPFUL TO FOCUS ON **ADDING**. ARE THERE PARTS OF THE ARGUMENT THAT SEEM UNDERDEVELOPED?

READ YOUR DRAFT AND THINK ABOUT WHAT QUESTIONS YOUR WRITING POSES -- YOU CAN EVEN WRITE THEM IN THE MARGINS.

DO ANY OF THESE QUESTIONS NEED TO BE ANSWERED?

IF SO, YOU MAY NEED TO DO FURTHER THINKING OR RESEARCH.

CHECK YOUR SOURCES CAREFULLY.

HAVE YOU CITED EVERYTHING THAT NEEDS TO BE CITED?

ARE YOUR IN-TEXT AND BIBLIOGRAPHIC CITATIONS IN ORDER?

REMEMBER THAT YOU SHOULD INVEST TIME IN READING YOUR OWN WORK CRITICALLY.

REFRAME

with

Luis & Cindy

Am I MISSING something?

HEY, CINDY, WHAT'S UP?

WRITING CENTER

WELL, I JUST MET WITH THE INSTRUCTOR FOR MY ART HISTORY CLASS, AND NOW I NEED HELP.

SEE, IT'S --

YANK!

WAIT A MINUTE...

...YOU'RE COMING TO THE WRITING CENTER FOR AN ART HISTORY PAPER?

YES, OF COURSE!

JONATHAN SAID WE COULD TAKE ANY KIND OF WRITING TO THE WRITING CENTER -- NOT JUST ENGLISH PAPERS.

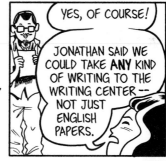

YANK BACK!

SIGH...

AND MY INSTRUCTOR SAYS I HAVE TO REVISE THE WHOLE PROJECT.

WRITING CENTER

FINE. HERE.

WRITING CENTER

WHAT'S **WRONG** WITH IT?

THERE'S NOT A **SINGLE** GRAMMATICAL ERROR IN THAT INTRODUCTION.

UHH...

MAYBE "SINCE THE DAWN OF TIME" IS A LITTLE TOO **GENERAL**?

WHAT ARE YOU **REALLY** WRITING ABOUT?

FROM THESE FIRST FEW SENTENCES, IT COULD BE PRETTY MUCH **ANYTHING**.

CAVE PAINTINGS. ISN'T IT **OBVIOUS**? IT SAYS RIGHT HERE...

WELL, YOU **DO** MENTION CAVE ART, BUT I CAN'T TELL WHAT YOU WANT TO SAY ABOUT IT. WHAT MAKES IT SPECIAL, OR UNIQUE?

THAT'S PRETTY MUCH WHAT MY INSTRUCTOR SAID.

WRITING CENTER

CINDY?

YOUR TURN!

SO, CINDY, WHAT ARE YOU WORKING ON?

MY PROJECT FOR ART HISTORY. THE INSTRUCTOR SAID IT "LACKED FOCUS."

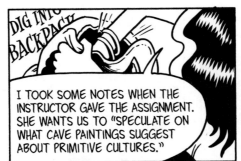

PREHISTORIC ART

Since the dawn of time, art has made the expression of ideas and feelings possible. This makes art a hugely important part of all human life. Art even appears in caves that were visited by ancient humans, and art remains an important part of basically every culture everywhere around the globe. Different people have different ideas about what makes art important or valuable, and about why works of art like cave paintings were created in the first place and how they can best be preserved for future generations. But many people agree that art is one of the ingredients that contributes to making life worth living. In this essay, I will examine the views of several important art historians about cave art and analyze where I stand on these questions.

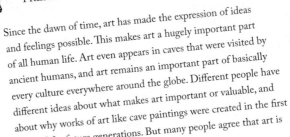

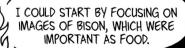

COMING UP IN THE NEXT EXCITING EPISODE OF **REFRAME**

"How does this LOOK?"

[pg. 267]

DRAWING CONCLUSIONS

The following assignments ask you to
think about your revision process.

1 Getting suggestions for improving your writing can be painful, even when your reviewer's intentions are good. Think about the kinds of feedback that you find most helpful and the ways you prefer to hear from peer reviewers (changes tracked in a document? verbal comments? a letter from the reviewer?). Compose an email to your peer review group outlining the kinds of feedback you prefer and the manner in which you want to receive that feedback.

If your class doesn't use peer review groups, consider starting one of your own. Most successful writers use them all the time!

2 Think about the last time you were in an argument -- and lost. With whom were you arguing? What was the argument about? If you could go back and change how you approached the argument, what would you do differently? Would you try a different rhetorical approach? Would you use different evidence to support your claims? Would you modify your primary claims to achieve a different outcome, such as a compromise?

Compose a short essay in which you describe the disagreement and analyze what was ineffective about your strategy and how you would modify it if you could replay the argument.

3

One fun strategy for "re-visioning" your work is to print out your writing assignment and then physically cut the paper into pieces. Cut out each paragraph, but also consider cutting individual paragraphs into two or more pieces. After jumbling up all the pieces, invite a reader to piece your work together again. You might find that another reader puts your work back together in interesting new ways.

Have introductory and concluding paragraphs changed places? Have body paragraphs moved around? Have paragraphs been rearranged? Reflect on whether the reorganization improves aspects of your writing. What changes do you want to keep?

4

Play "search and destroy" using the Find and Replace commands in your word processing program. If you notice (or a reviewer points out) that you rely too much on certain words or expressions, Find and Replace All of them with a word such as *BOOM!* You can then easily see where the overused material is so that you can change or delete it.

You can try a similar exercise if you discover that you use key terms or phrases too often in a single piece of writing. Use the Find command, but don't simply replace each word with a synonym; instead, consider how you can recast the sentence to avoid repeating the words.

bedfordstmartins.com/understandingrhetoric

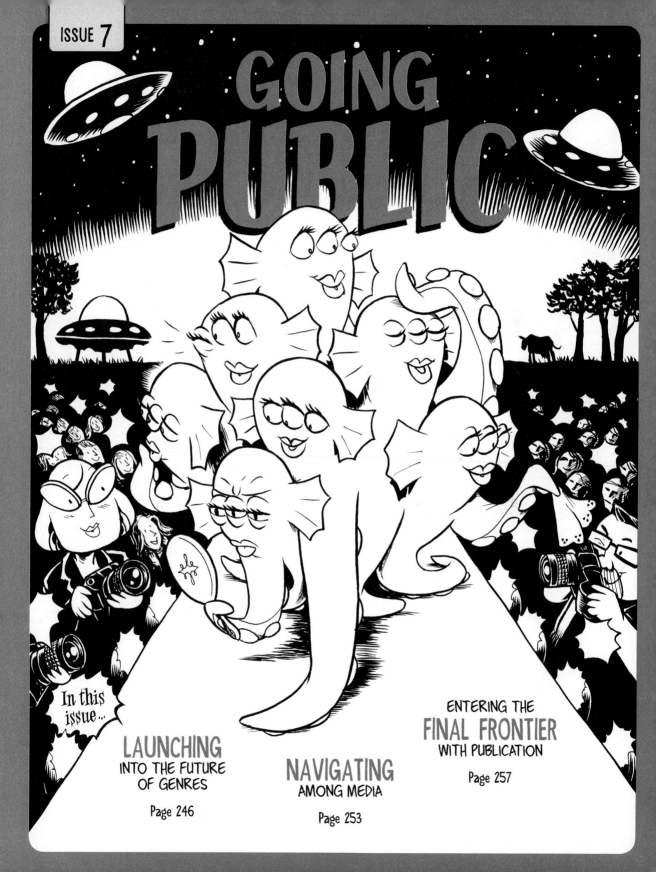

DIFFERENT GENRES CALL FOR DIFFERENT RHETORICAL CHOICES.

EVERYTHING WE SEE -- FROM WORD CHOICE TO DESIGN -- TELLS US WHAT TO EXPECT.

AUDIENCES FOR A NEWSMAGAZINE EXPECT TRUSTWORTHY STORIES, NOT INFLUENCED BY ADVERTISERS.

SO IT'S IMPORTANT FOR THE STORIES TO BE DESIGNED DIFFERENTLY FROM THE ADS.

BUT IN A SCIENCE FICTION MAGAZINE...

...TELLING THE ADS FROM THE ARTICLES PROBABLY DOESN'T MATTER AS MUCH TO READERS.

CERTAIN GENRES ARE COMMON IN ACADEMIC WRITING. YOU MIGHT WRITE JOURNAL ENTRIES OR EDIT MATERIAL FROM ORAL INTERVIEWS...

...OR COMPOSE LAB REPORTS FOR SCIENCE COURSES.

ACADEMIC DISCIPLINES OFTEN PREFER PARTICULAR GENRES THAT SET UP EXPECTATIONS FOR READERS.

PAN-GALACTIC TELECONFERENCE

BIOLOGY NEBULA

LITERATURE ASTEROID

ART GALAXY

A LAB REPORT, FOR INSTANCE, MAY BEGIN WITH BACKGROUND INFORMATION, A LITERATURE REVIEW...

...AND A METHODOLOGY SECTION THAT EXPLAINS HOW THE EXPERIMENTER PROCEEDED.

THIS CONVENTIONAL FORMAT PROVIDES INFORMATION THAT SCIENTISTS EXPECT TO KNOW BEFORE THEY READ THE RESULTS OF THE EXPERIMENT.

JOURNAL of Cool SCIENCE

LAB NOTES

AN ANALYSIS OF A **POEM**, IN CONTRAST...

...MIGHT NOT BEGIN WITH A SEPARATE BACKGROUND SECTION, BUT THE WRITER MIGHT BRING UP INFORMATION ABOUT THE POET'S LIFE OR OTHER CONTEXT WHEN ANALYZING PARTICULAR LINES.

PROVIDING THAT KIND OF INFORMATION IS A WAY FOR THE WRITER TO ANNOUNCE A PARTICULAR APPROACH TO INTERPRETATION.

HEY!

GORGO! NO!

SO, THERE'S A **METHOD** EVEN IN THE MADNESS OF POETRY ANALYSIS!

LEVEL of LANGUAGE

DESIGN

FORMAT

MEDIUM

SUBJECT MATTER

TONE

CHOICE

SOME GENRES THAT ARE DESIGNED FOR PARTICULAR PURPOSES AND AUDIENCES...

BUT THE FORMATS OF A LITERARY ANALYSIS AND A LAB REPORT WILL TYPICALLY BE VERY DIFFERENT.

...MAY SEEM PRETTY ALIEN TO OUTSIDERS.

HELP!

AND WHILE EACH OF THESE WRITING SPACES -- EMAIL, WEB PAGES, TEXTS -- CAN HAVE ITS OWN GENRE CONVENTIONS, EACH CAN ALSO ACCOMMODATE A WIDE VARIETY OF GENRES.

FOR EXAMPLE, BLOGS AND WIKIS ARE WEB GENRES THAT ARE ALSO COLLABORATIVE WRITING SPACES.

LIZ IS THE PRIMARY AUTHOR OF HER BLOG, *VIRTUALPOLITIK*, AND JONATHAN CAN MAKE COMMENTS.

ARTICLES ON WIKIPEDIA OFTEN HAVE MORE THAN ONE PRIMARY AUTHOR.

BARGE IN!

IN EACH CASE, THE GENRE ESTABLISHES EXPECTATIONS FOR HOW PEOPLE SHOULD CONVERSE ON THE SITE.

THE MOST INTERESTING AND ARTISTICALLY DECORATED CARDS GET POSTED ON THE POSTSECRET BLOG.

NOW THE IMAGES CAN BE SHARED...

...AND COMMENTED UPON...

...BY OTHERS.

AFTER A FEW YEARS, MODERATOR FRANK WARREN CREATED A BOOK.

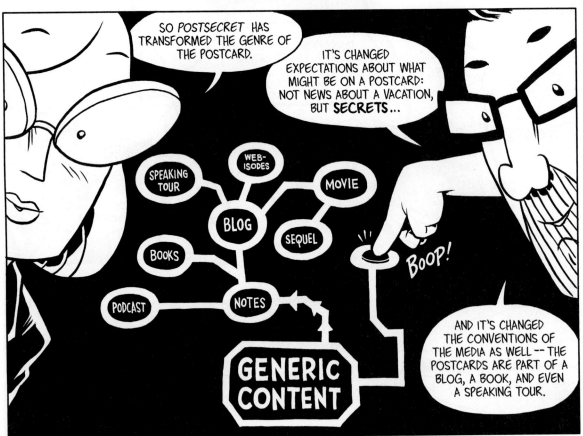

SO POSTSECRET HAS TRANSFORMED THE GENRE OF THE POSTCARD.

IT'S CHANGED EXPECTATIONS ABOUT WHAT MIGHT BE ON A POSTCARD: NOT NEWS ABOUT A VACATION, BUT **SECRETS**...

AND IT'S CHANGED THE CONVENTIONS OF THE MEDIA AS WELL -- THE POSTCARDS ARE PART OF A BLOG, A BOOK, AND EVEN A SPEAKING TOUR.

WHAT HAPPENS WHEN A BOOK BECOMES A FILM?

OR A TELEVISION SHOW BECOMES A VIDEO GAME?

WHAT DOES *PUBLISHING* MEAN, ANYWAY?

ENTERING THE FINAL FRONTIER WITH PUBLICATION

NO MATTER WHAT THE MEDIUM, GENRE IS ABOUT JOINING A CONVERSATION AND UNDERSTANDING THE RULES OF THAT CONVERSATION.

YOU CAN THINK OF GENRE AS THE STRUCTURE, THE SPACE OF CONVENTIONS, THROUGH WHICH WE COMMUNICATE OUR OWN IDEAS, IN CONVERSATION WITH OTHERS.

257

...IT ALSO **MOVES**.

IT CHANGES SHAPE, FORM, AND FUNCTION DEPENDING ON WHAT WE'RE COMMUNICATING, TO WHOM, AND HOW.

SOMETIMES SIMILAR IDEAS MAY BE PUBLISHED IN VERY DIFFERENT KINDS OF WORK.

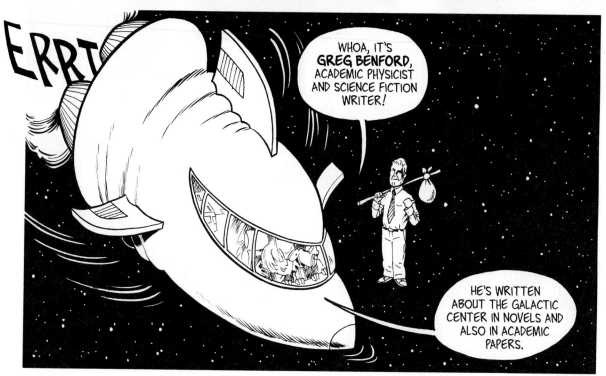

ERRT

WHOA, IT'S **GREG BENFORD**, ACADEMIC PHYSICIST AND SCIENCE FICTION WRITER!

HE'S WRITTEN ABOUT THE GALACTIC CENTER IN NOVELS AND ALSO IN ACADEMIC PAPERS.

259

...AND WITH INFORMATION DISSEMINATED AS QUICKLY AS IT IS PRODUCED AND CONSUMED --

WAIT, WERE YOU SPEEDING?

IT'S TRUE, MY FRIENDS.

TEXTUAL AND VISUAL MATERIAL IS CONSTANTLY ON THE MOVE...

...BEING RETASKED AND REPURPOSED FOR A VARIETY OF MEDIA...

...BUT YOU HAVE TO PAY ATTENTION TO WHAT YOU'RE DOING, OR YOU'LL END UP PULLED OVER TO THE SIDE OF THE INFORMATION SUPERHIGHWAY.

SPEEDING TICKET

YES INDEED, YOU HAVE TO PLOT YOUR COURSE CAREFULLY...

...AND MAKE SURE ALL THE GEARS OF YOUR MEDIUM AND MESSAGE FIT TOGETHER PERFECTLY, SO THAT YOUR WRITING DOESN'T...

...UHHH...

...ROCKET OFF IN THE WRONG DIRECTION...

bits

Ideas for Teaching Composition

Home About RSS

Taking Comics Seriously

Elizabeth Losh, Director of Academic Programs at Sixth College of the University of California, San Diego, and Jonathan Alexander, Professor of English and the Campus Writing Coordinator at the University of California, Irvine, are collaborating with artists Zander Cannon and Kevin Cannon of Big Time Attic on *Understanding Rhetoric: A Graphic Guide to Writing*, a forthcoming comic-style text for first-year composition students.

Learning to See Writing
posted: 2.13.12 by Elizabeth Losh and Jonathan Alexander

...'s post about co-authoring *Understanding Rhetoric: A Graphic Guide to Writing* mentions some ...he challenges of working on a graphic book. For ...one of the biggest challenges has been adapting ...thinking and composing in a different medium. ...eed, one of the lessons we have learned in the ...ocess is that we can't just think like "text" ...thors; we also have to begin to think visually. As ...e sketch out the chapters, panel by panel, we try to provide detailed visual cues for Kevin Cannon and Zander Cannon, our fabulous artists—who, in turn, not only modify our initial image directions and augment them beautifully, but have also challenged how we understand and use text in the graphic book form. (We'll be talking more about this process in our upcoming blogs.)

Jonathan

Along th... one of the earliest lessons we learned about our use of ...were initially relying too much on captioning and not ...n dialogue to carry the instructional weight of each chapter. That ...were thinking like the text-producing scholars that we are, and not ...he collaborative graphic authors we needed to be. We were constantly explaining rhetorical concepts, for instance, while ignoring how images and ...alogue—the principal features of the comic form—could be used to ...nvey our ideas about writing. Comparing initial drafts of the first several ...pters with their more recent revisions shows a steady move away from ...tioning to significantly more reliance on dialogue and visuals.

...ncomitant with that shift has been a shift in how we think about the ...oject and the processes we have to engage in to maximize our use of the

Blogs

> **Barclay Barrios** Emerging, A Blog
> **Joelle Hann (moderator)** Teaching Poetry
> **Nick Carbone** Tech Notes
> **Jack Solomon** Teaching Popular Cultural Semiotics
> **Gregory Zobel** Adjunct Advice
> **Traci Gardner** Teaching in the 21st Century
> **Jay Dolmage** Advice from How to Write Anything
> **Holly Pappas** Composing the FYC Course: Community College Style
> **Pitt Instructors** Teaching with Ways of Reading
> **Elizabeth Wardle and Douglas Downs** Write On: Notes on Teaching Writing about Writing
> **Nedra Reynolds** Resources for Teachers of Writing
> **Andrea Lunsford** Teacher to Teacher
> **Steve Bernhardt** Help Yourself
> **Susan Naomi Bernstein** Beyond the Basics
> **Donna Winchell** Argument and the Headlines
> **Elizabeth Losh and Jonathan Alexander** Taking Comics Seriously
> **Michael Michaud** The Paperless Writing Class
> **Nancy Sommers** Be... Nancy Somme...

Search F...

Recent...
> Manga...

AHH! YOU SEEM TO RECOGNIZE ALREADY THAT THE FORMATS AND GENRES THROUGH WHICH WE ENCOUNTER TEXTS ARE THEMSELVES IN MOTION, ACCOMMODATING NEW WAYS OF RECEIVING -- AND DISSEMINATING -- INFORMATION!

EXPERTS CALL THAT **REMEDIATION.**

THAT'S RIGHT!

TEXT IS ALWAYS ON THE MOVE.

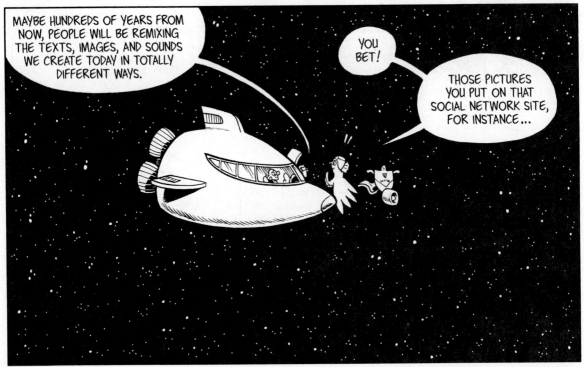

MAYBE HUNDREDS OF YEARS FROM NOW, PEOPLE WILL BE REMIXING THE TEXTS, IMAGES, AND SOUNDS WE CREATE TODAY IN TOTALLY DIFFERENT WAYS.

YOU BET!

THOSE PICTURES YOU PUT ON THAT SOCIAL NETWORK SITE, FOR INSTANCE...

REFRAME
with
Luis & Cindy

How does this LOOK?

HEY, LUIS.

HEY, CINDY!

HEY, CINDY'S MOM!

ISN'T THIS MEDIA LAB **AWESOME?**

YEAH, I'M DOING MORE AND MORE MEDIA PROJECTS FOR MY CLASSES, SO IT'S NICE TO HAVE ALL THIS SOFTWARE...

SO, WHAT ARE YOU GUYS UP TO?

I'M HELPING MY MOM LEARN TO MAKE PRE-SENTATION SLIDES.

SHE'S WORKING ON A PROJECT FOR **HER** WRITING CLASS.

COMPUTERS AREN'T MY THING, BUT I'M ACTUALLY HAVING A GOOD TIME ANYWAY...

YEAH, I'M WORKING ON A PRESENTATION TOO...FOR MY RESEARCH PROJECT ON FORCED MIGRATION.

I'M WRITING ABOUT PEOPLE WHO COME TO THE UNITED STATES BE-CAUSE THEIR LIVES ARE IN DANGER IN THEIR HOME COUNTRIES.

HEY, REMEMBER HOW I TOLD YOU THAT MY MOTHER LEFT VIETNAM AS A BOAT PERSON?

SHE CAME TO THIS COUNTRY BECAUSE OF FORCED MIGRATION.

HER UNCLE HAD ALREADY BEEN EXECUTED BY THE COMMUNISTS. HER OLDER BROTHER HAD BEEN A TRANSLATOR FOR THE U.S. MILITARY, SO THE WHOLE FAMILY HAD TO LEAVE.

I ALWAYS TELL MY DAUGHTER HOW LUCKY SHE IS.

I LIVED IN A REFUGEE CAMP WHEN I WAS HER AGE!

HMM...

REC

WOULD YOU MIND IF I INTERVIEWED YOU FOR MY PROJECT?

IT WOULD BE GREAT TO HAVE AN EYEWITNESS REPORT!

AND SO...

BUT HOW WILL YOU INCLUDE A VIDEO IN YOUR PAPER?

WELL...

...FOR OUR RESEARCH PROJECTS, WE HAVE TO WRITE A PAPER AND THEN CREATE A MULTIMEDIA PRESENTATION ON THE SAME SUBJECT.

LIZ WANTS US TO CHOOSE A SPECIFIC CASE STUDY, SO I COULD WRITE ABOUT FORCED MIGRATION FROM VIETNAM TO THE UNITED STATES.

Forced Migration Online: Resources f
Ongoing Study and Research

BY THE END OF THE TERM, WE HAVE TO COMBINE ALL OUR WORK INTO ONE COHERENT PROJECT...

...SO I THINK I'M GOING TO MAKE A WEB SITE WHERE I CAN POST MY PAPER ON VIETNAMESE REFUGEES AND ALSO LINK TO VIDEO AND IMAGES AND DOCUMENTS THAT I COLLECT.

AN INTERVIEW CAN BE A REALLY POWERFUL SOURCE.

CAROL, WOULD YOU TALK ABOUT WHAT IT FELT LIKE TO LIVE THROUGH FORCED MIGRATION?

I'D BE FLATTERED TO BE INCLUDED.

GREAT!

I'LL THINK OF SOME QUESTIONS, AND THEN WE CAN GET STARTED...

RESEARCH!

WRITE!

INTERVIEW!

EDIT!

271

I DUNNO... I'M SORRY MOM WAS UPSET, BUT IT SEEMS LIKE **CENSORSHIP** TO DELETE THE COMMENT.

REALLY*!?!*

I CAN'T BELIEVE YOU'D SAY THAT.

I KNOW, BUT THOSE VIEWS ARE OUT THERE...AND HIDING THEM WON'T MAKE THEM GO AWAY.

I THINK I'M GOING TO MENTION THIS INCIDENT IN MY INTRODUCTION, IF THAT'S OKAY WITH YOUR MOTHER.

LET ME EMAIL HER SO WE CAN TALK ABOUT IT.

ANOTHER WEEK LATER...

HEY, LUIS, CHECK THIS OUT.

MY MOM WENT TO THE MEDIA LAB AND MADE HER OWN VIDEO TO RESPOND TO THE COMMENT ABOUT HER INTERVIEW!

I KNOW THAT MY ADOPTED HOME, THE UNITED STATES, ENCOURAGES FREEDOM OF SPEECH...

...AND I'M DELIGHTED THAT BEING AN AMERICAN GIVES ME THE RIGHT TO TALK BACK TO THOSE WHO QUESTION MY CONTRIBUTIONS TO THIS COUNTRY...

WOW! GOOD FOR HER!

I KNOW. SHE ACTUALLY ROCKS SOMETIMES.

HIGH-FIVE!

NOW YOU CAN POST THE ORIGINAL VIDEO WITH BOTH THE ANGRY COMMENT AND HER VIDEO RESPONSE...

...LIKE A **DIALOGUE** -- BUT ONE THAT MAKES A REALLY EFFECTIVE ARGUMENT!

YOU KNOW MY MOM -- SHE ALWAYS GETS THE LAST WORD!

ha ha ha ha ha ha ha ha ha

273

DRAWING CONCLUSIONS

The following assignments ask you to think
about making your work available to audiences.

1 Moving your writing from one genre or medium to another
can be a powerful way to reexamine what you've
composed. Write or sketch a brief proposal to turn
an academic writing assignment into some other kind
of text, such as a brochure or an advertisement. What
choices help you communicate your primary ideas?

Reflect on what this "re-mediation" tells you about
what you chose to highlight. Are you making the same
main point (and making the main point equally clearly) in
both texts? Why or why not? What does your re-mediation
reveal about the academic assignment?

2 Reflect on your work by imagining how you might communicate your
ideas to different audiences or for different purposes. Take a piece you
have composed for an academic assignment and recast it for a different
audience. For instance, you might rewrite an analysis of a painting or
a lab report so that your parents or a younger sibling know what you're
talking about.

Reflect on how this
rewriting process
makes you rethink
your original piece
of writing.

3

Starting from the idea of a planet ruled by a cat, create works in at least two genres, choosing from these options or creating your own:

1) a one-page newspaper ad for a movie

2) a video trailer for a movie

3) a "short-short" or "flash fiction" story

4) a chapter of a comic book

5) an abstract for a scientific paper describing the imaginary planet

4

Make the work of assignment 3 public by posting a digital copy of it online. Send a link to your instructor along with a cover letter explaining your process of composition and reflecting on what you learned.

Did you collaborate with others in creating your content? Did you seek feedback on drafts? How closely did your method adhere to the approach outlined in this book? What parts of your process worked well, and what will you do differently the next time you tackle a similar project?

bedfordstmartins.com/understandingrhetoric

Acknowledgments

p. 16: *Casablanca* movie poster and still: Warner Brothers/Photofest.

p. 19: Human Rights Campaign logo: Courtesy of Human Rights Campaign.

p. 83: The New-York Historical Society. Frederick Douglass portrait. File PR-052.

pp. 103–09: Jacket design by Susan Mitchell, and pages from the *9/11 Report: A Graphic Adaptation* by Sid Jacobson and Ernie Colon. Copyright 2006 by Castlebridge Enterprises Inc. Reprinted by permission of Hill & Wang, a division of Farrar, Straus and Giroux.

p. 104: Cover of *9/11 Report:* Courtesy of W. W. Norton and Company.

pp. 173–74: Cover of Anya Kamenetz's *DIY U* © 2010 Chelsea Green Publishing, used with permission.

pp. 191, 193: Bettmann/Corbis.

pp. 209–13: Courtesy of JSTOR.

p. 268: Refugee Studies Centre/Oxford Department of International Studies.

GLOSSARY

INDEX

GLOSSARY

Analysis
A close examination of the parts of a text with the goal of interpreting it as a whole.

Argument
The primary purpose of a text, or the main claim it makes.

Assertion
A debatable claim.

Audience
The intended or accidental recipients of a communication.

Cause and effect
Tracing the reasons that led to an outcome, or anticipating the likely result of an event or circumstance.

Citation
The way the original source of a quotation, summary, or paraphrase is documented.

Comparison and contrast
Noting similarities and differences between two texts.

Composition
Creating a text in one or more media.

Conclusion
The end of a text that ties together its argument.

Context
The situation in which a text is created, including its creator, audience, purpose, medium, and genre, as well as other factors.

Credibility
The characteristic that makes a text believable.

Critical lens
A perspective or theoretical approach that provides a context for analysis.

Critical reading
An analytical approach to a text.

Discourse
Written or spoken communication, often characterized by its use in particular communities.

Ethos

The credibility or authority that a speaker or writer brings to a subject.

Evidence

The information used to support an argument.

Explication

Revealing or uncovering ideas that are not directly stated in a text.

Genre

A conventional format for presenting information and ideas.

Implicit messages

Ideas that are present in a text but not directly stated.

Integration

Weaving material from others' work into one's own text and adding commentary that explains the material's purpose and importance.

Interpretation

Using context and critical analysis to explain the meaning of a text.

Invention

Any technique (such as freewriting or brainstorming) for exploring new thoughts and ideas during the writing process.

Kairos

Awareness of the appropriate timing, occasion, or opportunity for a given rhetorical act.

Logos

Appeals to reason and logic in a text.

Medium (*plural,* Media)

Material that records, displays, stores, or spreads information.

Paraphrase

A detailed explanation of the contents of a source that rephrases the language of the original source.

Pathos

Appeals to emotion.

Peer revision *or* Peer review

The process of seeking feedback on a text from a classmate, colleague, or friend.

Glossary

Plagiarism
Presenting the work of another as one's own, whether accidentally or deliberately.

Primary source
A work that presents a firsthand account of an event or a time.

Purpose
The aim of a communication.

Quotation
Direct repetition of material from a source.

Reflection
In writing, an analysis of a completed project that considers what the writer learned during the writing process.

Remediation
Revising a text that appeared originally in one medium so that it is effective in another medium.

Revision
The process of rewriting to improve a text, often by viewing it from different perspectives.

Rhetoric
The practice or study of effective communication.

Rhetorical analysis
Examining how, what, and why a given text communicates.

Secondary source
A work that describes, analyzes, or interprets a firsthand account or original work.

Summary
A brief, general restatement of the content of a source.

Surface errors
Distracting mistakes in grammar, punctuation, or spelling.

Synthesis
Putting information from multiple sources together to make one unified meaning.

Text
In rhetorical terms, any communication in any medium—including print books, films, Web content, slide presentations, Facebook posts, and so on.

Thesis
The main idea that a text develops.

Tone
The attitude that a text conveys to an audience.

Visual literacy
The ability to analyze elements of a visual text.

Voice
In writing, the way a writer expresses the person behind the words.

Writing process
The steps writers take in composing a text, which can vary greatly from writer to writer and from situation to situation.

INDEX

Index

More good stuff for students online.

Free.

Visit the *The Student Site for Understanding Rhetoric* at bedfordstmartins.com/understandingrhetoric

- Deleted panels and early versions of the book for comparison and contrast

- Behind-the-scenes videos to meet the creators of *Understanding Rhetoric*

- Sample student projects to hint at what's possible

- Additional topics for research and writing

- Background information to learn more about what's in each chapter

- Help with creating your own comics

- Tutorials on writing topics